Bob Snodgrass
Publisher

Gary Carson
Photo Editor

Linda Overbay
Editor

Brad Breon
Managing Editor

Darcie Kidson
Publicity

Randy Breeden
Art Direction/Design

Dust jacket design by Jerry Hirt

Dust jacket photos by Ernest Withers

Production Assistance: Michelle Washington, Sharon Snodgrass, David Power, Jeremy Styno

Photography courtesy Ernest Withers, Gary Carson and Bob Guthridge and Memphis/Shelby County Public Library

Published by Addax Publishing Group, 8643 Hauser Drive, Suite 235 Lenexa, Kansas

Printed and bound by G.S.America, Memphis, Tennessee, United States of America.
DISTRIBUTED TO THE TRADE BY ANDREWS MCMEEL PUBLISHING, 4520 Main Street, Kansas City, Missouri 64111-7701

ISBN: Cloth 1-886110-18-2
ISBN: Paper 1-886110-20-4

Library of Congress Cataloging - in - Publication Data

Worley, William S.
     Beale Street : crossroads of America's music / by William Worley.
          p. cm.
     Includes bibliographical references.
     ISBN 1-886110-20-4 (pbk.). —ISBN 1-886110-18-2 (hard.)
     1. Beale Street (Memphis, Tenn)—History. 2. Beale Street
(Memphis, Tenn.)—Pictorial works. 3. Memphis (Tenn.)—Buildings,
structures, etc. 4. Memphis (Tenn.)—Social Life and customs.
5. Popular music—Tennessee—Memphis—History and criticism.
6. Afro-American musicians—Tennessee—Memphis—History. I. Title.
F444.M575B439 1997
976.8' 19—dc21   97-35857
                                                              CIP

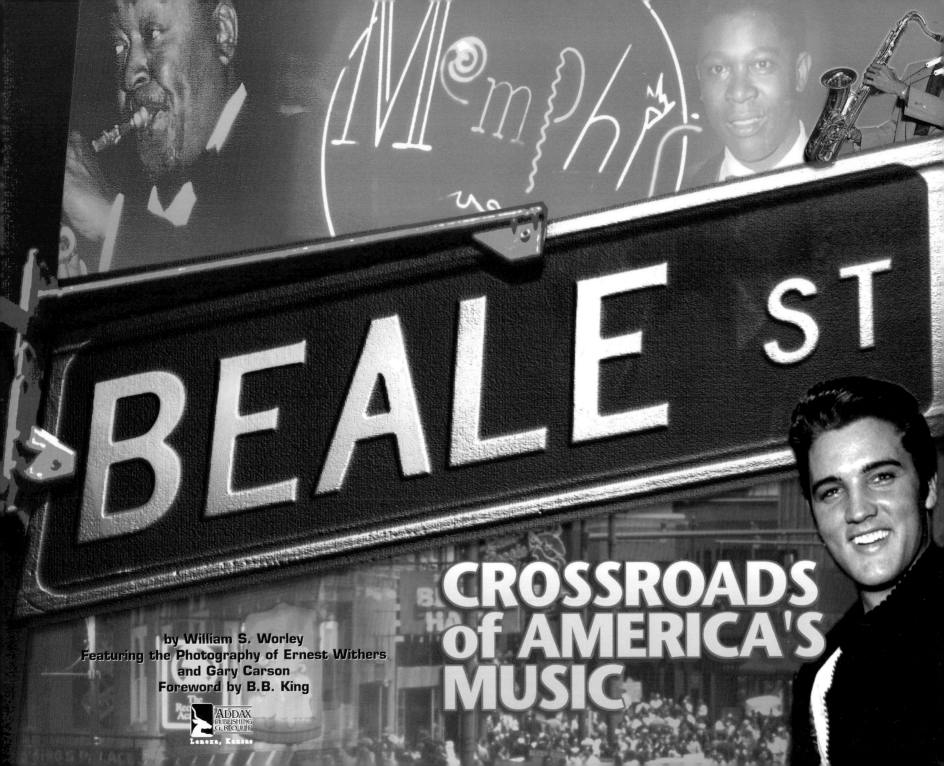

BEALE ST

CROSSROADS of AMERICA'S MUSIC

by William S. Worley
Featuring the Photography of Ernest Withers
and Gary Carson
Foreword by B.B. King

ADDAX
PUBLISHING GROUP
Lenexa, Kansas

Table of Contents
Beale Street

Introduction
John Elkington

When we began the redevelopment of Beale Street in 1983, the street was a facade hiding in its rich heritage. There were no neon signs, no music and no young musicians looking for their big break. The street itself was decayed and only two establishments, A. Schwab's and Hudkins Hardware, were still open for business.

We set out to redevelop the street by establishing three main goals: 1) Return commerce to the street, 2) Make Beale Street the center for music and entertainment in the mid-south region, and 3) Make Beale Street the place in Memphis where blacks and whites could work and play together.

The initial development team consisted of a very young and energetic group of people. Robert Boyd, a twenty-four-year-old African-American, who had recently graduated from Brown University, was the energy behind this group. Cynthia Hamm came on board to develop a marketing strategy that would carry us through the first 10 years. Her associate, Davis Tillman, developed our festival concept and introduced the Labor Day Music Festival and the New Year's Eve Bash on Beale. Cato Walker, the son of a legendary Beale Street musician, directed our entertainment, while Joe Sabatini, as Chief Operating Officer added stability to our young organization. Then there is Al James, who for 15 years has made sure Beale street operated right. Without him, there would be no new Beale Street. Steve Keltner, my partner at the time, was very supportive and was the one who encouraged me to go "after" Beale and redevelop it.

Along the way, there has been Don McMinn, Mike Ritz, Cookie Johnson, Judy Douglas, Dianne Glasper, Mark Bishop, Mike Hjort, Sonia Walker, Sherry Adams, Paul Gurley, Shannon Black, Toni Holmon Turner, Ricky Pette, Rev. James E. Smith, Randall Catron and Calvin Taylor who have all added to Beale Street's success and added their own personality to the development. Finally, without the leadership of Mayor Dr. W. W. Herenton, we could not take Beale Street to the next level.

In addition to the efforts of the development team, business owners took an equal risk to be a part of Beale. John Robertson was our first serious operator, my dear friend Preston Lamm, the legendary Silky Sullivan, Mike Glenn and Marsha and Jerry Burt are just a few of the proprietors who have brought the blues back to Beale Street.

This book examines all the changes over the years. From it's opening in October, 1983 to today, as we measure the new Beale Street's direction not in small steps, but in great strides. Today, B.B. King's, Willie Mitchell's Rum Boogie, The New Daisy Theater, Hard Rock Cafe, Elvis Presley's Memphis, Alfred's, Blues City Cafe, Silky O'Sullivans, Memphis Music, King's Palace and the Black Diamond all represent Beale Street.

Finally, this book traces the history and culture that Beale Street strives to maintain. It illustrates the history of Beale Street and its stars - B.B. King, Muddy Waters, Rufus Thomas, Howlin' Wolf, Ruby Wilson and so many others.

Beale's rebirth did not happen by miracle or magic, but by the efforts of hundreds of *Memphians*.

Beale Street, Crossroads of America's Music chronicles the history and the pride of this great street. Put a CD on and walk down Beale. Feel the blues capture your imagination.

Foreword
B. B. King

Beale Street is my street. I don't say that because I own it, even though I do have a club on one nice corner. Beale Street is mine, because Beale Street is the Blues. The Blues is something that a person feels in their heart. If they can feel it, I can sing it or play it or at least get inside it.

I remember my first visit to Beale Street like it was yesterday. One of the first things I saw were black people and white people shopping in the same stores on Beale Street. A lot of the merchants tried to help in a friendly way. I just had not seen a situation before, where blacks and whites could get along like they seemed to on Beale Street. What I see today, when I'm in town long enough to notice, is a place where White folks and Black folks have a good time, make a living, and enjoy the music all along Beale.

I guess my most memorable day on the street came in the 1950s when I first took my own band out on the road. The picture that Ernest Withers took of us that day is in this book. That was my independence day. This didn't mean that everything went perfect after that. There were lots of bumps in the road, but from that day

to this, I've had a band, I've played Lucille, and I've enjoyed hundreds of thousands of fans all over the world. Where did it all begin—right there on Beale Street.

I've played all over the world, but I never will forget something that Nat D. Williams said years ago. This was a long time before they copied his idea for a song about New York City. What Nat D. said was, "If you can make it on Beale Street, you can make it anywhere." That wasn't meant for anybody more than it was for me. I never had a history class from Nat D., but he taught me some lessons about Beale Street, about life, and about myself I'll never forget.

Enjoy the book. The pictures are great. The story is important. Come see Beale Street, while you're there, come by my place, and tell them "B.B. sent you" and remember as long as there's a Beale Street, there'll be the Blues.

Mansions on Beale Street, 1880s

Located mostly on the stretches of Beale east of Wellington [Danny Thomas] Boulevard, these large old houses provide substance to the reality of Beale Street as a one-time residential street for moderately wealthy whites. By the 1880s, the transition to almost exclusively Black residential neighborhoods around Beale was already underway. These particular houses were located near the intersection of Beale and Lauderdale Streets.

Beale Street. The very name conjures up images of music, commerce, food and drink - all nestled in a few blocks of downtown Memphis, Tennessee. The music is the blues and its offspring: rock 'n' roll along with rhythm & blues; the commerce includes souvenirs, Fiesta-ware dishes, and almost everything in between; the food and drink are ever-so-plentiful in bright, shiny clubs and restaurants. This is the New Beale Street, reborn out of the ashes of reform politics, desegregation, urban renewal, and repeated failures.

"Come what may, there will always be a Beale Street, because Beale Street is a spirit ... Beale Street is a symbol ... Beale Street is a way of life ... Beale Street is a hope."

- Nat D. Williams,
***Memphis World*, November 30, 1945**

The origins of Beale Street go back to the 1840s, when it was a principal avenue of the separate community of South Memphis. Although Memphis had been incorporated as a city in 1826, it didn't consolidate with South Memphis until 1849. At that time, the eastern half of Beale, from Wellington (now Danny Thomas) to Manassas, was an upscale residential street mostly occupied by white families. But by the 1850s, the lower blocks of Beale near the wharf had begun developing as a commercial site for businesses catering to the free black population of Memphis.

The roots of the old Beale Street of song and legend really lie in the cholera and yellow fever epidemics of the 1870s and '80s. Those catastrophes created opportunity for migrating former slaves and their children - the opportunity to participate in the development of a multi-racial commercial center that would serve the needs of Memphis' growing black community. The opportunity was born of necessity - blacks had nowhere else in Memphis to go to buy the goods and services they needed. Main Street and Union Avenue were off limits as places of commerce for Memphis African-Americans. This left Beale Street to emerge as the commercial center for Memphis' black community, where they could frequent its groceries, saloons, restaurants and cafes.

The name "Beale" appears to have been selected by the antebellum developer of South Memphis, a white man named Robertson Topp. According to Topp family legend, the name was that of a United States military leader of the 1840s. But recent efforts to identify either a General or Admiral Beale or "Beal" (the early spelling on some maps) were unsuccessful. Thus, the most famous street in Memphis and one of the best-known in America seems to have been named for a now unknown person.

For almost 50 years, Beale Street was officially Beale Avenue. In 1908, the outgoing city council gave a nod to Progressive Era orderliness by declaring that all north-south thoroughfares were streets while east-west connections became officially known as avenues. But in 1955, Memphis-born comedian Danny Thomas preserved the traditional name when he asked the city commission to change it back officially to Beale Street. Most folks on the Street never bothered to call it anything else.

Beale Street's nickname, "the birthplace of the blues," has been credited to W. C. Handy, a bandleader who was writing music in Pee Wee's Saloon on Beale Street in 1909. Handy wrote part of the music for "Mr. Crump," a tune that helped political boss E. H. Crump win the mayoral election in 1909. That song was later expanded and transformed into "The Memphis Blues."

The Rev. A. D. "Gatemouth" Moore
Beale Street Profile

When you talk to the Rev. Moore, quietly smoking a cigar in front of the Center for Southern Folklore, you don't realize immediately that this is a man who has seen it all. He grew up in Kansas where his mother worked in the house of a wealthy Topeka family.

His singing career began in a way more like that of W. C. Handy than like blues legends Furry Lewis or "Bukka" White. In the early days, "When Irish Eyes Are Smiling" was more frequently in his repertoire than any blues song. In 1939, W. C. Handy was invited to return to Memphis from his adopted home in New York City for the high school Blues Bowl football game. The old bandmaster asked A. D. Moore to sing the "Beale Street Blues" while riding in car in front of the Booker T. Washington High School band. A.D. Moore became "Gatemouth," and for the next 10 years, achieved success for his blues numbers as well as for white musical standards.

Ten years later, at a big night club in Chicago, Gatemouth came out to sing blues. Instead, he found himself singing an old gospel tune, "Shine on Me." He left the stage and returned to the church

upbringing of his youth. Ordained to preach in the African Methodist Episcopal tradition, he ministers today in Mississippi congregations such as Yazoo City.

On special festival weekends, though, you can see and hear him at the Folklore Center - that wonderful mix of coffee house, beer garden, library, and cultural haven now located at the corner of Hernando and Beale. He'll sing, maybe preach a little, smoke a cigar now and again. Mostly he talks … and listens. Usually one of his children is nearby, just to make sure Daddy Moore is doing all right.

Even if he grew up in Kansas, even if he sang more white pop tunes than blues, even if he came to the ministry in mid-life, the Rev. A. D. Moore has lived and seen much of the last 50 years of Beale Street history. His life weaves together those varied elements of blues, gospel, and more that have sustained the Street and its residents through hard times and now in somewhat more comfortable times. Like Rufus Thomas, B.B. King, and Ernest Withers, the Rev. A. D. "Gatemouth" Moore is a real Beale Street person.

Nat D. Williams

Beale Street Profile

When former Memphians Margaret McKee and Fred Chisenhall began researching their excellent *Beale Black and Blue*, they relied on the memories and documents of Nathaniel Dowd Williams. They were fortunate enough to have begun their quest for aspects of Old Beale's soul when Nat D. and many of the bluesmen still lived. Sadly, it took a good deal longer to get a publisher, and Nat D. was not in good health when the book came out in 1981. He died in 1983.

Nat D. Williams may well have influenced more lives on and near Old Beale Street in its declining days than any other soul. He taught so many in his Booker T. Washington High classroom, where, as recounted by former student Richard Jones, he delighted in telling American history from the black man's point of view, which was not exactly the acceptable interpretation to the more accommodationist school administration. Nat D. developed the uncanny knack of knowing when the principal or a more conservative colleague was going to wander by or into his classroom. As naturally as taking a breath, he could switch, for their benefit, from a description of the founding fathers as slave-owners to an eloquent recounting of their heroic stands for liberty.

He did this only partly to cover himself. Nat D. Williams knew that American history is full of irony. Thomas Jefferson could advocate freedom for white men passionately while keeping company with his slave Sally Hemmings.

As McKee and Chisenhall point out so clearly in their Beale Street book, Nat D. did more than teach in the classroom. He wrote columns for the *Memphis Globe* and for out-of-town black newspapers across the country. On Tuesday nights in the '50s particularly, he played straight man emcee at the Amateur Night competitions at the Palace Theater while Rufus Thomas led the buffoonery. Nat D. became the first black deejay on WDIA when it announced its rhythm & blues format in 1949.

What the earlier writers did not know was the degree to which Nat D. influenced the lives of many such as Ernest Withers, Richard Jones, and others who have helped document the transitions in the life of this fabled Street called Beale.

It's way too much to say that Nat D. Williams personified Beale Street; its personalities are much too varied for that. What he did do was respect the Street and to call upon his friends and neighbors to be the best they could be on their own terms. Nat D. never imposed outside white standards on his Beale Street brothers and sisters. He called them to what he believed was a higher black standard - one that knew the jiving and knew the truth - the deep-down, hard-to-get-at truth that only the blues revealed fully.

The Early Beale Street

Prior to the Civil War, when Beale Street and South Memphis were residential areas for middle- to upper-income whites, blacks worked as their house servants. But the end of the war brought increasing numbers of African-Americans to live on or near Beale Street, as many former slaves fled to the relative freedom of the city rather than stay on the plantations.

Memphis suffered greatly during the post-epidemic years after 1878. Because blacks in Memphis suffered a lower death loss during the cholera and yellow fever epidemics than did the whites, the African-American population continued to increase. Also, more black Memphians stayed in town during the epidemics because they had nowhere else they could go.

By 1890, African-Americans comprised approximately 50 percent of the area population. Where white Memphians focused their economic attention on the downtown area from Union to Jefferson Streets along either side of Main, by this time, black Memphis now had its own commercial center - Beale Street. The transition in racial composition ran from the 1850s through the 1880s and, though never complete, Beale Street became known as "the Main Street of black Memphis" by the 1890s.

Robert R. Church had much to do with the development of Beale as a black business center. Church began his commercial career running a saloon on Beale Street in the 1860s. During the post-Civil War era, he carefully bought up property on and near Beale, establishing businesses and selling property to blacks and whites who wished to commercially serve the growing African-American community in south Memphis. Late in his life, Church established the Solvent Savings Bank primarily to serve Beale Street businesses and residents.

In 1899, another great contribution by the Church family became one of the most important historical institutions on Beale Street. Church Park opened that year with six acres of open park space around the First Baptist Church of Beale Street. It included a 2,000-seat auditorium designed to serve the needs of the Beale Street community, since the city of Memphis refused to provide either parks or meeting spaces for almost half of the city's population. Church Park was privately owned, but never legally racially segregated in the way the city-owned parks were until the 1960s.

Over three decades, until its replacement in 1929, Church Park Auditorium served as the scene of school graduations, political gatherings, dances, and even conventions or church meetings too large for any of the nearby sanctuaries. The Church family replaced the old auditorium in 1929 with a smaller community center that still accommodated some of the largest black crowds in the city.

Next door to Church Park, The First Baptist Church, Beale Street, was an early institution that met many of the needs of the former slaves. It evolved into the mother of all black Baptist congregations in Memphis and the mid-South, and, according to some historians, it was the first black Missionary Baptist Church in the United States. The First Baptist Church, Beale Street, continues its record of preaching and service to the surrounding community into the 21st century.

Businesses along Beale Street have always had a rainbow hue of ownership. Church, his son, Robert, Jr., and other African-American businessmen have always owned a portion of the commercial ventures on the Street. Beginning around 1900, Irish and Italian business owners were prominent, and from the 1920s through the 1970s, a significant number of Beale Street businesses, including dry goods stores and pawn shops, were owned and operated by Jewish business people as well.

In one instance - the construction of the Beale Street Market in 1898 - a city public works project brought about greater interaction among Beale Street African-Americans and new immigrants to the United States. The city planned the market as the site for farmers and shippers to bring fruits, vegetables, and meat for sale to wholesale companies and private individuals. In the days before supermarkets, grocery stores did not stock perishable items such as these. By 1910, a good-sized Italian population (although comprising only a tiny percentage of the total city population) centered their business activities in or near the market building.

Ironically, the Beale Street Market became an early casualty on the Street. It was torn down in 1928, with the site converted to become the location of W. C. Handy Park on Beale between Third and Rufus Thomas Boulevard.

The areas around Beale Street, particularly on its south side, teemed with humanity housed largely in one-story, narrow, "shotgun" houses. So narrow that they would not permit hallways, the houses got their name from the idea that a shotgun shell fired through the front door would exit the back door without touching a wall because of all the interconnecting doorways. Frequently, shotgun houses contained only two or three rooms.

These were working-class black neighborhoods in which the women and men both had to work outside the home in order to make ends meet. While that pattern became common in white America after the 1960s, it was always true for black families because wages in the jobs open to blacks always brought substantially less income than those held by whites.

Saturday night on Beale Street was the only time that hard-working

John "Red Johnny" Brown in Front of His Former Tavern

For decades during and after World War II, John Brown administered Red Johnny's Tavern at Beale and Hernando, the site originally housing Pee Wee's Saloon at the turn of the century. This institution included the normal barroom space, but it also had a meeting or party room. Here Brown stands in front of the historical marker telling of W. C. Handy's role in the development of the blues.

Some years after this, Handy's widow explained that her husband only did the orchestrations of the Crump (Memphis) Blues at Pee Wee's. He used a rented office elsewhere on Beale Street in which to compose and write lyrics, since it was impossible for him to do this work at their small shotgun home, filled with six small children.

African-Americans could blow off a little steam. The clubs and bars stayed open as long as legally allowed. Jam sessions by blues musicians echoed far into the night, the entertainment ranging from a fancy party with private band at the Elks' Club to the wild abandon of the Hole in the Wall and other gambling/drinking establishments.

W. C. Handy recalled those pre-World War I days on Beale Street in his 1941 autobiography, *Father of the Blues*. Most specifically, he remembered the goings-on around Pee Wee's Saloon on the southeast corner of Fourth and Beale.

"Just inside Pee Wee's entrance door there was a cigar stand. A side room was given to billiards and pool. In the back room there was a space where violins, horns, and other musical instruments were checked by free-lance musicians who got their calls there over phone number 2893. Sometimes you couldn't step but for the bull fiddles. I've seen a dozen or more of them in there at one time.

"Through Pee Wee's swinging doors passed the heroic figures of an age that is now becoming fabulous. They ranged from cooks to waiters to professional gamblers, jockeys, and race track

A W.C. Handy Blues Band, 1918

Even after he had removed himself and his family to New York City, W.C. Handy continued to book blues combos for various occasions. During his Memphis years [1903-1916], Handy booked as many as six different bands under his name on weekends for different functions. In most cases, as in this instance, Handy himself did not appear with the bands. The handwritten inscription on the bass drum reads: "To my esteemed friend, Mr. R.R. Church, with my best wishes, W.C. Handy, June 8, 1918."

men of the period. Glittering young devils in silk toppers and Prince Alberts drifted in and out with insolent self-assurance. Chocolate dandies with red roses embroidered on cream waistcoats loitered at the bar. Now and then a fancy girl with shadowed eyes and a wedding-ring waist glanced through the doorway or ventured inside to ask if any had set eyes on the sweet good man who had temporarily strayed away."

Around the turn of the century, Pee Wee's was the favorite watering hole for Handy and other musicians. The owner, Italian immigrant Vigello Maffei, was willing to provide the all-important telephone connection, which was usually answered by Maffei or his brother-in-law/partner, Lorenzo Pacini. They would take messages about potential band gigs and post them on a bulletin board.

Handy described a lively night on Beale when he remembered composing the "St. Louis Blues":

"I rented a room in the Beale Street section and went to work. Outside the lights flickered. The chitterling joints were as crowded as the more fashionable resorts like the Iroquois. Piano thumpers tickled the ivories in the saloons to attract customers, furnishing a theme for the prayers at Beale Street Baptist Church and Avery Chapel (Methodist). Scores of powerfully built roustabouts from riverboats sauntered along the pavement, elbowing fashionable browns in beautiful gowns. Pimps in boxback coats and undented Stetsons came out to get a breath of early evening air and to welcome the young night. The pool hall crowd grew livelier than they had been during the day. All that contributed to the color and spell of Beale Street mingled outside, but I neither saw nor heard it that night. I had a song to write."

William Christopher Handy is probably best remembered as the composer of the "St. Louis Blues." In spite of the name, it was written about life on Beale Street in a little rooming house located just off the thoroughfare.

After the excitement of Saturday night came Sunday morning. Most Beale Street women found their way to First Baptist Church, Beale Street, to nearby Clayborn Temple of the African Methodist Episcopal Church, or to one of several of other nearby black churches. Many of their husbands attended with them. A few black

families attended St. Patrick's Roman Catholic parish. Mostly, though, Italian families with homes and businesses in the neighborhood went to early Mass at the Catholic church.

Thus, Beale Street served as a community center, not just a commercial thoroughfare. People lived along it or, more frequently, on side or parallel streets. They worshiped in churches along the Street or nearby as well. They bought their groceries and buried their dead in establishments operating on Beale as well.

Music echoed up and down the street almost any hour of the day or night. Without question, Saturday night was when musicians played loudest and longest. From the 1890s through the 1940s, the music was mostly the blues. More particularly, it was the Mississippi Delta blues.

Beale Street clubs afforded musicians mostly friendly surroundings and an interested, but not wealthy, clientele. Establishments such as the Hole in the Wall, The Monarch, The Yellow Door and others provided a stage and an audience for persistent young blues players coming to town.

How did these clubs continue to exist in spite of local and national prohibition? Law enforcement was lax along Beale Street from Main east to Wellington (Danny Thomas). Mayor Boss Crump made sure that the club owners understood how much he did for them, and, in turn, club owners paid handsomely into the white Democratic Crump machine in order to stay in business. Beyond available liquor, gambling and prostitution also abounded along Beale. Beale Street's famous night (and day) life existed because the powerful Crump thought it was good for business and good for Memphis.

There was some opposition to the blues in Memphis, however, based on both race and class discrimination. Whites boycotted it because the performers were black and the songs resounded of poor rural backgrounds.

Even within the black community, there were many who opposed the blues and everything connected with the music. Understandably, the ministers of the community opposed the late hours, the alcohol, and the loose sexual behavior, to say nothing of the gambling, that went on in and around the blues joints on Beale

Party on Beale Street, 1950s

Odd aspects of Tennessee liquor regulation became one of the things which kept some aspects of Beale Street alive. This party group had to bring its liquor with them to one of the Beale Street clubs. The club made its money by selling "set-ups" or soft drinks which could be used as mixers with the alcohol. The alcohol itself had to be purchased in a sealed "package" at a neighboring liquor store by the party-goers. The goal of the legislation was to prevent alleged abuses of "liquor-by-the-drink." Sadly, the result frequently was that alcohol consumption increased as purchasers sought to empty their bottles while at the party.

Street. Black Christianity saw itself as the defender of high moral behavior in the community, and the blues halls and juke joints tended to foster the opposite kind of behavior. Additionally, money spent by men in the joints never made its way to the collection plate on Sunday mornings. Sadly, too, money spent on the dice horn never made it home to help feed and clothe the family.

Middle-class blacks comprised another group within the black community that opposed blues singers and the joints they frequented. Although a small minority of the overall population, these modestly prosperous professionals looked down on blues players and blues joints as both rural and low-class in their appeal.

Middle-class blacks were just as susceptible to the snobbery engendered by such opposition as anyone else. Obviously, their disdain could not be considered a racist response, but it very definitely coincided with the class bias exhibited by middle- to upper-income whites over the same issue. To a black doctor or attorney, the blues were a reminder of all that he or she sought to avoid or get beyond.

The whites' double standard about what they considered the degenerate nature of Beale Street entertainment became apparent on Thursday nights

West Memphis Gambling Joint, 1950s

After the death of Boss Crump in 1954, reform politicians tried to complete the elimination of drinking and gambling joints along Beale Street which Crump had begun. Instead of getting rid of the problems, the gamblers simply moved across the Mississippi River to West Memphis, Arkansas. While Ernest Withers could have snapped this photo in any one of a dozen or more gambling joints right on Beale Street in the late 1940s, he had to go "across the river" to get the shot a decade later. Dice games proved particularly popular both on Beale Street and in West Memphis. The dice were not thrown as in "craps," but shaken in a horn on the table surface. When released, bets were settled based on the final resting position of the ivories. The use of the horn was supposed to reduce fraud through use of loaded dice or other tricks.

from the 1930s into the 1950s. One of the regular events of Beale Street were the Thursday night "Midnight Rambles," conducted in the Palace Theater for whites. "On six nights a week, Beale Street is a Negro street, but on the seventh (Thursday) it belongs to the white people. White people of all classes, some in overalls, others in evening dress, attend what are locally called 'rambles.' Here they see 'scantily clad brown beauties dancing across the stage ... .' " The theater was operated by the Italian families Pacini and Barrasso primarily for a black audience, but they discovered that whites would pay well for "a night on Beale Street," seeing what the mostly male audience was not allowed to witness in other sections of the city.

One Beale Street event that has continued into the late 1990s began during the Great Depression. Concerned that the only celebration of the role cotton played in the lives of all Memphis citizens was a whites-only Cotton Carnival, Dr. R. Q. Venson decided in 1936 to start a "Cotton Makers Jubilee" parade for blacks. Schools, churches, and civic organizations within the black community competed on the march down Beale Street for prizes and honor.

Marching Group, Cotton Makers' Jubilee Parade, 1940s and 50s

While the A.Schwab sign is clearly displayed, the most important thing happening here is the marching of a black youth organization in the annual Cotton Makers' Jubilee Parade.

White Memphis held an annual Cotton Carnival patterned after Mardi Gras in New Orleans. Understandably, black Memphians felt both left out and exploited, since over the years, African-Americans plowed, planted, chopped, and picked most of the cotton throughout the South. Thus, a different celebration came together along Beale Street. To point out their own heritage, this event was called the "Cotton Makers' Jubilee," the highlight of which was a long parade down Beale Street by bands, floats, marching groups, and other organizations. The tradition continues to the present.

Memphis' Boss Crump had a great deal in common with another political dictator of the times, Tom Pendergast of Kansas City. Pendergast encouraged vice and gambling in the heart of Kansas City's black neighborhoods at 18th and Vine Streets, understanding that white Kansas City did not overly object to wide-open amoral conditions so long as the custom of racial segregation was followed and the activity did not spill over into white neighborhoods too frequently. Crump acted in the same manner in Memphis.

1939 and 1940 were years of change in Memphis. In response to state investigations of his potential manipulation of black voters, Crump decided to pressure white wards to deliver the spectacular majorities necessary to express Crump's political will in the city and across the state of Tennessee. When Tennessee prohibition ended in 1939, Crump's ability to control aspects of city life through the bootlegger network came to an end, so he looked for new sources.

Crump found he could rely on money supplied by white businessmen to keep his machine operatives in line, no longer needing the rake-offs and protection payments from Beale Street club owners. In 1940, E. H. Crump closed down the old speakeasies, gambling dives, and havens for prostitution which had become famous.

The results of Boss Crump's about-face gradually became apparent. In 1939, the white political leader changed the name of the one black community center and park in the city from Church Park to Beale Avenue Park, confiscating the park land from the Church family for back taxes. Prior to this time, most businessmen operated under an unofficial policy that allowed them to defer paying any property tax until they sold a particular piece of land. Crump's hand-picked city officials chose to revoke Church's right to defer payments, and thus grabbed the land. Not until the 1950s and the end of the Crump era were black

Beale Street Lady in Front of a Rooming House Sign, 1930s

This Depression-era scene on Beale Street shows one part of the residential aspect of Beale Street. Because of its fame among sharecroppers in Mississippi and western Tennessee, Beale Street was the first place many rural African-Americans would come when they arrived in the big city - Memphis. The word had been passed over the decades: For blacks in Memphis, Beale Street was where it was happening.

Of course, most of the new arrivals did not have enough money to stay in the somewhat fancier hotels along the Street or intersecting side streets. Rather, they would consult with this lady or others offering "Rooms for Rent" in the general area. As soon as they could, these new arrivals would try to find something more permanent. But first, they had to find a job, and in Depression Memphis, jobs were difficult to locate. Some might stay only a few nights and then hop an Illinois Central freight train bound for Chicago or a Frisco freight for St. Louis or Kansas City. Sadly, these other towns did not have many jobs available either.

1958 View of Beale Street at Rufus Thomas on the eve of Urban Renewal

Looking west through the Hernando intersection, a declining but physically intact Beale Street is evident. Handy Park stands where the trees are visible on the right. The Gallina Building is intact behind its imposing facade just beyond the bend at the Third Street intersection. The large multi-storied building in the center was the Randolph office building, razed in the 1960s to create a space for Memphis Gas, Power and Light building at Second and Beale.

Even in decline, signs along the Street express aspects of its vitality. The Harris Department Store provided a wide variety of items for sale to area residents. John Brown's pool room served as an entertainment center next door to Red Johnny's Tavern (Falstaff sign), owned by the same John Brown. Public telephone signs indicated locations of pay telephones for the use of many of the Beale Street residents who could not afford to have in-home phone connections. The height of the Gallina Building above its neighbors long created a billboard site filled here by an advertisement for Old Crow bourbon.

Note the number of people on the sidewalk and the automobiles parked along the Street. A certain amount of prosperity is evident from the presence of a brand new 1958 two-tone Chevrolet parked at the corner next to the entrance to Harris' Department Store. At that time, parking was at such a premium that parking meters stood as regulators of the available spaces.

Memphians able to get the park renamed after the man who originally developed it before the turn of the 20th century.

With the onset of World War II moderate prosperity came back to Beale Street which mitigated some of the previous insults. Possibly the best description of 1940s Beale Street, in the midst of its last heyday before the 1980s, comes from the blues-singing uncle of B.B. King, Booker T. Washington White:

"Shoot, I used to sleep on Beale. We used to play in that park (Handy Park) on Beale. Every Saturday night, if you wanted to find anybody, you go to Beale Street at that park. This where they at. Just like we do now when we's in the small towns, we had our hat down, let them throw the money in it. The police used to come stand there, listen to us play. I knowed the police many times to turn around, chunk us a half or quarter.

"If there ever was a good time, so help me God, there was good times on Beale Street. People from everywhere was coming to find out about that place; people you see there you ain't ever seen before in

your life. You know, Beale Street was a joint street, it was a drag street, it was a drawing street."

"Piano Red" Williams agreed: "In the old days on Beale you could say it was never nighttime. They just stayed open from dawn to dawn. Everything was lively."

The Depression had dealt the entire city of Memphis a severe blow, but it hit nowhere harder than in the black community. The absence of the Solvent Savings Bank, which had failed in the late 1920s, combined with hard times to drive many blacks out of business.

After the war, white city officials and business leaders encouraged other whites to move into formerly black-run businesses or to take over long-time locations run by whites who had befriended and helped their Beale Street customers. Pawn shops took over from grocery stores; liquor stores replaced neighborhood cafes; some store fronts were just boarded up, even though the population density around Beale Street remained high compared

Blind Man Begging on Beale Street, 1960s

This well-dressed gentleman for years occupied a spot near Hernando and Beale Street. Each morning he appeared with his folding stool, cigar box, knapsack, and tin cup. He sat and held out the cup to passers-by, asking for donations. He always left a coin or two in the tin cup from the previous contribution in order to have something to rattle in the cup when he heard footsteps. The worn white canes and the non-matching socks give evidence to the man's financial problems while the suit and summer straw hat might make someone think he was well-off enough already. The unidentified gentleman simply believed in dressing as well as he could for his encounters with people along Beale Street.

to the city as a whole. The pattern displayed a concern for profit above service and for extracting the maximum amount of financial benefit possible.

Then came a series of blows that almost destroyed Beale Street entirely. The first change came with efforts toward federal government-subsidized urban renewal. Under the guidelines of this program, government agencies could buy up "blighted areas" for pennies on the dollar, destroy the structures remaining, and turn the empty land over to developers who could construct new office buildings, commercial structures, or housing on the site. The idea, once again, was to make the unprofitable areas profitable, even if those areas had to be destroyed in order to make the plan work.

Urban renewal was a national program, but it struck Beale Street especially hard. Several buildings on the street dated from before the 1920s, but many had fallen into disrepair. In the 1950s, when urban renewal gained its preeminence, there was little thought of preserving historically significant districts, even if someone in the white Memphis power structure had decided that Beale Street was important - which they did not. "New Is Better" was the slogan of the era. Bulldozers razed countless buildings along and near Beale.

Another factor came into play. In 1954, school desegregation became the law of the land with the U.S. Supreme Court decision in Brown vs. Board of Education. Memphis school officials resisted desegregation as long as possible, but by the early 1960s, it was inevitable. The response of many white Memphians was to move out of the city. They moved ever eastward, south and north where black population densities declined into nonexistence. Understandably, those African-American families who had the means bought or rented much of the housing vacated by the fleeing white population.

This meant that the numbers of people living in the immediate area around Beale Street declined substantially. Part of the decline occurred when housing structures were bulldozed for urban renewal, but a lot of the exodus represented black flight into parts of the city with affordable and better-quality housing than had previously been available to blacks at any price. With fewer people living nearby, Beale Street businesses lost even more customers. By the 1970s, boarded-up storefronts became the rule rather than the

exception, and venerable entertainment centers such as the Palace Theater disappeared under the wrecker's ball.

One of the earliest post-World War II efforts towards Beale Street redevelopment began in 1959 with a pronouncement by then-Mayor Edmund Orgill, who announced that "Beale Street would be converted into a major tourist attraction for Memphis and America." He placed the effort under the control of the Memphis Housing Authority, a 24-year-old public agency charged with creating and upgrading housing for the poorest citizens of the city. Of course, the Housing Authority decision makers were all white.

At the outset, Beale Street renewal became Memphis' fifth post-war redevelopment project, covering 167 acres ranging over 14 blocks on or near Beale running east from the Mississippi River. A housing survey conducted by the Housing Authority at that time concluded that 625 buildings existed in the new redevelopment district. Of those, the surveyors estimated that 570 of the structures were in substandard condition.

In 1966, a different image for a new Beale Street formed in the minds of planners at the Memphis Housing Authority. They announced plans to convert "drab Beale Street into a glittering jewel, complete with its own revolving-tower restaurant at the Mississippi River, a riverfront freeway, high-rise apartments, a plaza along Beale, and a huge, covered commercial mall."

Then came the King assassination and the ensuing recriminations among city leaders. Following closely on the heels of this civic and personal disaster, the election of Richard Nixon changed federal government priorities for city rebuilding. There just weren't enough sources of money to afford the estimated $200 million this ambitious plan required. By the mid-1970s, it was dead in the water.

Also in 1966, the National Park Service bestowed Historic Landmark status, with Interior Secretary Stewart Udall presiding at the ceremony. U.S. Representative George Grider of Memphis attended to celebrate the results of his intensive lobbying effort to accomplish the designation. Even Memphis-born entertainer Danny Thomas sat on the platform with the widow of W. C. Handy. Handy was a focus of the celebration because of the presence of Handy Park in the newly designated Historic Landmark area.

Richard Nixon on Beale Street

In 1960 as he battled John F. Kennedy for the presidency, Nixon visited Beale Street under the sponsorship of long-time Beale Street Republican, Lt. George W. Lee. It was part of the early effort toward developing a "southern strategy" for the Republican party. In this case that meant recruiting support in Memphis' Black community.

By 1970, the mood was still cloudy for Beale Streeters. Long-time bluesman Booker T. Washington White commented, "If there ever was a good time, so help me God, there was good times on Beale. But the good times are gone for good."

Joe Raffanti, owner of the Midway Liquor Store at Fourth and Beale, commented in 1973, "They keep tearing buildings down and boarding them up, but nothing is ever built." At the same time, Abe Schwab commented to the *Commercial-Appeal* newspaper, "Nobody lives within a half-mile of here now." He estimated that between 8,000 and 10,000 people had moved out or been relocated since the mid-1950s, and he expressed doubt that anything could be done to bring Beale Street back to its former self: "If they try to build something like Pee Wee's Saloon, I don't think they can do it."

Things got so bad by 1978 that city officials discovered official maps of the city printed between 1973 and 1977 simply omitted the four liveliest blocks of Beale Street. Sadly, no public official or citizen with enough clout to be heard even noticed the error. That same year, the *Commercial-Appeal* commented editorially about Beale Street and the city of Memphis as a whole: "The crumbling walls of

Beale and Main, about 1970

The fate of Beale Street was very much undecided around 1970. Pawn shops and loan companies comprised the most numerous occupants of the street. Liquor stores such as the one on the corner came in a close second as the most plentiful type of store. The buildings in the foreground were replaced by the 1980s with the new modern home office of the Tri-State Bank, Beale Street's own financial institution.

Beale Street won't last much longer without help; neither can a city divided against itself. If ever a community was in need of good news, this is it. And news of Beale Street's (projected) restoration heralds the opportunity at least to bring the community together - an opportunity it cannot afford to turn down." This was 10 years after the assassination of Dr. Martin Luther King, Jr. brought home to Memphians and the nation how divided the city really was.

White rock musician Jim Dickenson asserted in a recorded rock documentary and tribute titled "Beale Street Saturday Night" that the late March incident on Beale Street when Dr. King led his last civil rights march was really a small affair, with some looting and a large amount of police over-reaction. Nonetheless, "it was used (by the city) as an excuse to tear down Beale Street."

Beale Street was the site of Dr. King's last civil rights march in 1968. Scheduled to proceed from Clayborn Methodist Temple on Hernando, down Beale to Main and east to City Hall, the march stopped short of its goal. Rowdy hangers-on began smashing windows of stores on Beale Street. The police moved to halt that activity, and the entire march reversed itself back down Beale toward the Methodist Temple.

Martin Luther King at the Lorraine Motel in 1966.

The Palace Theater Faces Urban Renewal

Just before its destruction in 1973, the Palace stood in the shadow of its former self. Pee Wee's Saloon (later Red Johnny's) is already gone. In its heydays from the 1920s through the 1950s, the Palace was the show theater of Beale Street.

The Barasso family and their relatives, the Zerillas and Pacinis, owned almost all the theaters on Beale Street - the Savoy, Pastime, Daisy, and Grand as well as the Palace. To provide a continuing source of entertainers, F. A. Barasso formed the Theater Owners' Booking Association (TOBA) in 1909, which developed into the network for black vaudeville and musical entertainers throughout the eastern half of the United States. More than 40 theaters in Kansas City, Oklahoma City, Chicago, New York, Washington, D.C., Memphis, and points in between participated in this booking service. The owners liked it because it provided them with a reliable stream of talent. Many of the jazz musicians, comedians, and dancers disliked it equally as much. They believed they were being exploited by low wages and bad living conditions for the profit of largely white theater owners.

The entertainers probably were correct; however, it is equally possible that many fewer jobs would have existed had not the Barassos and other owners joined together to provide a regular route of venues. The entertainers frequently called the organization "Toby," or assigned more colorful words to fit the actual acronym. The circuit did not survive the hard times of the 1930s and the Great Depression.

Another Palace tradition had just as much impact nationally as the TOBA arrangement. Tuesday nights from the late '20s through the late '50s were Amateur Night contests. For most of that period, Nat D. Williams, a local newspaper columnist and Booker T. Washington High School history teacher, served as master of ceremonies. Rufus Thomas, who later billed himself as the "world's oldest teenager," provided comic relief.

The contests were a come-one, come-all affair. Some screening of acts took place, but some of the worst were allowed to perform, if only to let the "Lord High Executioner" do his thing. If performers were bad enough to get booed by the crowd, they were supposed to leave the stage. Some did; some didn't. Those who stayed got "shot" by the executioner, who leaped from wings with a pearl-handled pistol containing blanks.

One of the most famous "finds" at the talent show came late in its career when Riley King came to Memphis from Mississippi late in the 1940s. In the beginning, he suffered the boos and even the Lord High Executioner at Amateur Nights, but he kept coming back - a little more polished each time. By 1950, he was good enough to get invited by Nat D. Williams to participate on a show on WDIA radio, Memphis' first R & B station. In the process he picked up the nickname, "Blues Boy" King. That quickly got shortened to just "B.B." The rest is history.

Dr. King planned to lead another march in Memphis early in April 1968 but was felled by the assassin's bullet at the Lorraine Motel before that happened. Thus, Beale Street figured heavily in creating the circumstances surrounding his death.

Memphis state historian Jack Hurley has noted that in 1968, more than 300 families and more than 450 single persons still lived on or near the main part of Beale Street. By 1979, the number of resident families had fallen to zero. The only new housing was a high-rise public housing unit, named for long-time Black dentist, Dr. R. Q. Venson.

This project, dedicated to the service of the elderly, was constructed at Beale and Danny Thomas. Of all the antebellum and 1880s houses that used to line the noncommercial sections of the street, only the Hunt-Phelan house, just east of Danny Thomas, remained. "The city has spent $26 million over the past 20 years to recreate the look of Hiroshima in 1946 (along Beale Street)," commented Hurley. "Only in Hiroshima, we did it a lot quicker."

Larry Payne Casket in Clayborn Temple, March 1968

Lying in state in the sanctuary of Clayborn Temple, African Methodist Episcopal Church, on Hernando just south of Beale, Larry Payne was the first victim of the unrest ensuing from Dr. Martin Luther King's Beale Street march. National Guardsmen thought Payne was returning to one of the public housing projects with loot from Beale Street. One frightened young Guardsman believed Payne had a knife as the Guardsman approached. The "peacekeeping force" shot and killed Payne in his own doorway. Such were the tensions of the period that the killing was ruled "justifiable homicide." No evidence surfaced that Payne posed any physical threat to the National Guard or to his neighbors.

Looting Following Beale Street March, March 29, 1968.

The Beale Street March, led by Dr. Martin Luther King, Jr., was supposed to go all the way to City Hall on Main Street. Because young men, not part of the march at all, started breaking windows along Beale Street, the march leadership chose to end the march short of its destination. Approximately the same time, Memphis police decided to intervene on Beale Street. The result was chaotic as this picture demonstrates. Property damage was generally limited to plate glass windows. It turned out to be the last civil rights march led by Dr. King before his assassination a few days later.

1968 Sanitation Worker Strike—A Scene on Beale Street.

In a somewhat unlikely photo, a young White woman walks Beale Street with several Black men protesting the wages and working conditions endured by Memphis' Black sanitation workers. This was the same union recognition struggle which drew Dr. Martin Luther King to Memphis in late March and early April, 1968. The young woman's sign read "We Are Together, Once and For All." The Black man's sign appears to have read, "Dignity for All, I Am a Man" which was the slogan of the Sanitation Workers' Union.

Beale Street Comes Back ... Finally

The phenomenal rebirth of Beale Street began in 1982 with the assumption of management for the project by Beale Street Management, now known as Performa Entertainment Real Estate, Inc. John Elkington, who has headed the development since that time, noted that in 1982, only two businesses continued to operate between Second and Fourth in the heart of the Beale Street district. Only one survived the decade. Only A.Schwab continues its more than a century-long tradition of selling dry goods from a familiar storefront on the Street.

In early 1983, before any restored or compatible new construction opened under Beale Street Management leadership, the Tennessee legislature passed one of the critical measures necessary for transforming Beale back to its much earlier position as an entertainment center for the city. State Senator John Ford, from Memphis, shepherded through a bill that allowed alcoholic beverage purchasers to buy a drink between Second and Fourth Street on Beale and legally carry it on the Street. Controversial at the time, the new rule creates the sense that one can move freely from club to club, band to band, and not have to "drink up" in a hurry. Particularly on festival weekends, such a rule allows visitors to the Street to

enjoy the music and spirit in a more relaxed, open-air environment.

Another important decision made in 1983 proved important for bringing Beale back. Just as it had operated wide open seven days a week in its various periods of strength, Beale Street would be open for business on Sundays as well. This came shortly after the Street officially "reopened" on October 10 with several new businesses in place. Particularly at festival times, but also during other parts of the year, this decision has made possible full weekend utilization of the entertainment district. Shelby County Mayor William Morris commented at the grand opening celebration: "Beale Street used to be a place where people were there because they were separated from the rest of the community. But today people are here for a different reason - to be together rather than separated." The new inclusive approach to Beale Street redevelopment took hold.

A critical battle, necessary to retaining the significance of the Street, came in 1987. Since 1966, Beale Street retained its designation as a National Historic Landmark by the National Parks Service. Because of the reconstruction and demolition required to make Beale Street viable again, many in Memphis and across the United States argued that the Historic Landmark status should be voided. Elkington and his Beale Street Management team fought hard to retain the valuable designation. In spring 1987, a special board of the National Park Service voted to continue the Historic Landmark status for the section of Beale between Second and Fourth Streets.

All kinds of special events and ongoing negotiations proved necessary to help keep the final, successful phase of Beale Street's long comeback road alive. In April 1987, the Rev. A. D. "Gatemouth" Moore emceed an open air "Night at the Palace Theater" on the site of the razed building near Hernando and Beale, where such entertainers as Rufus Thomas, B.B. King, Bobby Blue Bland, and Johnny Ace got their start at the Amateur Night competitions. The actual theater disappeared amidst all the "urban renewal" destruction of the early 1970s.

Across the street the new Daisy Theater was built in the early 1950s. Possibly its

Isaac Hayes at David Porter's Walk of Fame Note Ceremony

proudest day came in 1958 when the world premiere of "The St. Louis Blues," Hollywood's version of W. C. Handy's biography, opened there. It was a gala occasion to celebrate the Memphis roots of the one-time Beale Street composer and bandleader.

The most lasting Handy memorial beside Handy Park, is the Handy House. In 1985, it was moved from its original site a few blocks off the Street to its current location at Fourth and Beale. Its importance is two-fold. First, it brings to mind the role of the bandleader and songwriter in popularizing aspects of the Memphis blues. Secondly, the house is an example of the "shotgun" type of residence occupied by thousands along and near Beale Street from the 19th century to the present.

Another growing attraction along Beale Street is the Walk-of-Fame with its notes that now dot the sidewalks between Second and Fourth. Among the earliest

John Elkington (left) of Perfoma Entertainment Real Estate Company and B.B. King (right).

Two men are among those most responsible for the return of Beale Street as an entertainment and shopping area for Memphis. Since 1982, John Elkington and his staff have worked tirelessly to create and recreate Beale Street into the premier attraction it is in the late 1990s. B.B. King's establishment of his own club at the corner of 2nd and Beale provides a critical anchor to the north end of the historic district. King has always sworn allegiance to Beale Street and all it embodies.

honorees were W. C. Handy, Memphis Slim, Nat D. Williams, Furry Lewis, and B.B. King.

Guiding principles for the redevelopment of Beale Street were laid down publicly in a 1988 speech to the Phoenix Club in Memphis when John Elkington summed up the goals of Beale Street redevelopment: "In dealing with Beale Street, we made three promises: (1) We would return commerce to the street. (2) Beale Street would become the music and entertainment center of the community. (3) It would become a place where there would be no barriers, real or imaginary, and where citizens of all races would be welcome."

At the conclusion of the speech, Elkington commented on the progress of Beale Street and on the lack of progress in race relations in other parts of the city:

"For any of you who have visited Beale Street on any weekend night, you can see it is one of the few places where whites

Rev. James E. Smith, Joe Sabatini, B. B. King and Sid Sidenberg

and blacks can gather. It is a place where, hopefully, we can foster an understanding in the community. Because the ultimate problem and the ultimate test of success rests with the development of the community in other areas. It's in that economic growth area I talked about at the first press conference. It is breaking the cultural poverty that Mayor Morris has spoken of. We must address in the community the problem of the homeless and the more serious problem of lack of decent housing and education."

What Elkington was saying is true of all American cities, just as it is true of Memphis. If, indeed, the successful redevelopment of Beale Street can have even some of the impact in the other areas outlined here, it will become a model for America. That would be a real legacy for the Street and all its inhabitants in the past, present, and future.

Where did Memphis music come from? At its base, it came from rural communities, tiny towns and county seats in the Mississippi Delta, in western Tennessee, and northeastern Arkansas. It came from black churches, juke joints, medicine shows, and even black minstrel shows. It came out of everyday experiences, out of work, out of dances, out of the vagaries of human relationships.

The real question is not so much: "Where did it come from?" as: "Where did it come together?" For that, there's an easy answer - Beale Street.

In his book *It Came From Memphis*, author Robert Gordon says that The Music "hit" three times in Memphis - the blues, from the turn of the century to the present; rock 'n' roll by way of Sun Records in the '50s; and rhythm & blues from the '40s onward but particularly as expressed on Stax Records of the 1960s.

less profound. For people like Dewey Phillips on the Memphis airways, Beale Street was where it was at. For newcomers like Sam Phillips (no relation to Dewey), Beale Street spoke of rhythms and sights he only dreamed about in Muscle Shoals, Alabama. More than that, to Sam Phillips, Beale Street stood as a symbol for blacks and whites - a place where blacks could be somebody and whites could learn to work side-by-side with them. Sam Phillips recorded Elvis Presley's first record, "That's All Right," at Sun Studios, and Dewey Phillips played it on the air on WHBQ before the vinyl was even pressed.

Rock 'n' roll is what happened when whites tried to sing the blues. Rhythm and blues is what happened when blacks speeded up the blues and added special touches. Stax Records became one of the foremost rhythm and blues recording companies in the early 1960s, mostly with R & B artists like Otis Redding, Rufus and Carla Thomas, Isaac Hayes, and

It isn't hard to see the connection between Beale Street and the blues. Rural black folks came to the city to find work and a little less oppression. Their music traveled with them in their heads, their hands, and, most of all, their hearts. B.B. King's pilgrimage to Beale to find his cousin, "Bukka" White, in 1946 is a prime example.

The Beale connection to rock 'n' roll is a little less obvious - but no

more. Just to confuse things a bit, Robert Gordon observed that Stax's recording artists often turned out to be the same bands that played to all-white audiences in West Memphis and to black audiences on Beale Street or elsewhere in Memphis.

So, in Memphis, the music is blues, rock, and R & B. None of it would have happened if it hadn't been for Beale Street.

Live at the Club Paradise

Sunbeam Mitchell's Club Paradise Hosted a Swinging Newcomer, 1950s

As the Blues became Rhythm and Blues in the hands of talented Black Musicians, many found at least temporary fame on the stage of Mitchell's successor to Club Handy—Club Paradise. This unidentified group was backing the vocal stylings of a young male singer. If the names of the participants have slipped from the memory of Beale Streeters, the liveliness of their music has yet to fade. Club Paradise served to expand the influence of Beale Street musicians into other parts of the Memphis musical scene in that period.

The Blues Originated in the Mississippi Delta

The blues is both a simple and a complex music form. It is simple because of its straightforward lyrics and phrasing; complex because of the degree to which it builds on a whole array of earlier music forms in the rural South.

Most people consider a delta to be the place formed by a river when it spills into the ocean. The Mississippi River has such a delta all right, but it is below New Orleans and not heavily populated. In the northern half of Mississippi, between Memphis and Vicksburg, there is another kind of delta. It consists of the eastern watershed of the Mississippi River and the western watershed of the Yazoo River. At no point is there really a dividing ridge between the two valleys. The land lies so flat and low that the rivers tend to flood into each other's valleys whenever a good deal of water comes down either one.

The result is a very fertile, yet dangerous, pie-shaped region with enormously productive soil deposited over the millennia by countless floods. Not heavily settled until after the Civil War when sharecropping became the rule of land use, the Mississippi Delta region became the most intensely rural and most concentrated African-American-populated section in the entire United States.

Huge cotton plantations evolved in subdivided form. Owners partitioned off hundreds of 40-acre plots for black sharecroppers. The white plantation owners not only controlled the country stores, where sharecroppers and their families were required to shop, the owners also set up the cotton gins to which the sharecroppers had to take their small crops for processing and marketing. The gins paid prices set by the plantation owners, not by the Cotton Exchange in Memphis, and the plantation general stores sold goods or extended credit only to those sharecroppers in the good graces of the owners.

Place names like "Stovall," "Sherard," "Ferrell," and "Sessions" appeared on Mississippi state maps alongside county seats like Tunica, Hernando, Clarksdale, and Indianola. These were really the names of the landlords of the plantations and stores at the county road crossings, not the names of actual communities.

The small communities gathered around small churches and schools established by the sharecroppers themselves. In later years, the white-controlled county governments established county school boards and superintendents to control both black and white schools. School terms were different because black children were expected to help in the fields from March through at least October. Plus, the black schools usually got hand-me-down textbooks and minimal facilities.

In normal conditions, the black sharecroppers could never hope to break even when marketing their meager crops. Because almost no whites would sell land to blacks even if the latter somehow scraped together enough money to purchase the land they tilled, there was little hope for blacks to achieve any kind of economic independence in the rural plantation system.

Over time, this reality led many African-Americans to flee their sharecropper plots and find protection in the relative anonymity provided by growing cities like Memphis or even Chicago, taking with them the knowledge and appreciation of the blues musical form as developed in the Mississippi Delta and the rural South. Although many were glad to be out of the grinding grip of the sharecropping system, they missed the personal contacts, family relations, and informal music of their old home areas.

The blues came to Beale Street, then, in the 19th century. Nobody knows for sure, but it was probably when the first freed slaves arrived from the Mississippi River plantations such as the one owned by Joseph Davis, Jefferson Davis' brother, at Davis Bend, Mississippi, between Greenville and Vicksburg. The blues were in people's heads and their hands, but at the time nobody thought to write the music down.

That had to wait until at least 1909, when black bandleader William C. Handy, newly arrived in Memphis from Clarksdale, Mississippi, was given the difficult political assignment of beating the drum for a white reform candidate mayor E. H. Crump. Reform in Memphis usually meant closing down bars and joints along Beale Street, at least for awhile, and Handy knew that wouldn't be popular with most Beale Streeters.

Handy had discovered how well blues style songs went over with black audiences around Clarksdale and Coahoma County in Mississippi, so he composed a melody that took the repetitive form of the blues he had first heard in his youth around Florence, Alabama. Mostly, it was an instrumental piece, but for the campaign Handy added the following lyrics:

> "Mr. Crump won't 'low no easy riders here.
> Mr. Crump won't 'low no easy riders here.
> We don't care what Mr. Crump don't 'low
> We gon' to bar'l house anyhow -
> Mr. Crump can go and catch hisself some air."

It's quite likely that Mr. Crump didn't get all of the innuendo of the lyrics, which basically said that Beale Streeters might vote for Crump, but they weren't going to stop going to the barrel house beer joints. The last line indicated that he could "go jump in a lake," to use another euphemism.

The fact was, the words didn't matter to the whites - they loved the tune. Blacks liked the tune fine - and also understood the lyrics. As it turned out, Crump's devotion to reform lasted about as long as most Beale Streeters expected. As soon as the election was over, he announced that he had no intention of allowing the state of Tennessee to enforce its newly enacted prohibition law in the city of Memphis, a position he held until forced from office after his third re-election in 1916. The state authorities planned to remove him if he didn't resign or enforce the Tennessee

The Blues That Made Beale Street Famous

To support the first mayoral election of Edward H. Crump, W.C. Handy was commissioned to write a rousing number to attract attention to Crump in the Black community of Memphis along Beale Street. The result was "Mr. Crump's Blues" in 1909. A few years later Handy scored the number and included the not entirely complimentary lyrics [to Mr. Crump]. The sheet music publisher wanted a title so Handy renamed it "The Memphis Blues."

The Blues form had been around for decades before Handy scored this number, but "The Memphis Blues" marks the first time that the familiar rhythms and rhyming scheme were produced as band or piano music.

Prohibition Act. It might appear, then, that the Beale Streeters who listened to Handy's "Crump Blues" and voted for the future political boss in his first big election, got exactly what they bargained for - a reprieve and a champion, at least for the moment.

Crump's ouster in 1916 occasioned one of Handy's next big blues hits, "Beale Street Blues." The closing lines in this sequel to "Mr. Crump" tell the sad story:

"Goin' to the river, maybe bye and bye -
Goin' to the river, and there's a reason why -
Because the river's wet, and Beale Street's done gone dry."

As it turned out, Handy's fears about the dire results of enforced Prohibition were a bit overblown. At Pee Wee's Saloon, for instance, they simply turned out the lights at the appointed hour for compliance. Five minutes later, Pee Wee's speakeasy reopened with soda and ginger ale on the shelves instead of whiskey. It continued operation in that manner with customers supplying their own "beverages" to go with purchased "set-ups" throughout national prohibition and the extended Tennessee ban on alcohol which lasted until 1939.

By the 1920s, blues clubs existed all along Beale Street and into the neighboring area. Some of the singers had migrated farther north to St. Louis or Chicago or even New York City, as did W.C. Handy himself in 1918. They followed their people and sang to them in bars and clubs not unlike the "juke joints" with which all were familiar in the Delta country.

A series of changes in local restrictions in the years before World War I brought about a change in the composition of the population on or near the Street. Memphis instituted segregated streetcar service in 1906; and the state of Tennessee passed a state-wide prohibition law against alcoholic beverages in 1909. While Mayor E. H. Crump succeeded in preventing the enforcement of Tennessee Prohibition laws until 1916, the trend toward segregation and restriction was clear to many middle-class and professional African-American families. A significant number led the movement to the North that after World War I came to be called "The Great Migration."

All these segregation measures created ripple effects out across the surrounding countryside. In Clarksdale, Mississippi, 50 miles south of Memphis, additional segregation restrictions during the war era became the impetus for a large-scale movement of middle-income blacks to Memphis in the 1920s. In the larger city, these black professionals, many of them trained at Alcorn A. & M., tended to take over the roles vacated by the Memphis professionals who had left for St. Louis, Chicago, Detroit, and Cleveland.

In the mid-1920s, enough southern blacks had migrated north and held down jobs that paid for the necessities, plus a little extra, to create a demand for recordings of the music from "home." Always on the alert for new markets, recording companies began to set up sessions in the northern cities, producing what came to be known as "race records." Labels such as Victor, Vocalion, Columbia, and others recorded literally hundreds of songs and musicians during the middle and late 1920s.

No extensive recording facilities existed in Memphis in the 1920s, so the national companies sent engineers and portable equipment for use in hotel rooms or anywhere enterprising engineers could set up and attract the local talent. Sometimes the blues musicians traveled north to meet the engineers and producers in the more professional surroundings found in St. Louis or Chicago.

Regardless of the recording location, the Mississippi Delta blues, most frequently as shaped through time in Memphis and around Beale Street, became a time-honored musical form alongside jazz in northern cities. Blues and jazz clubs flourished from Chicago through Detroit, Cleveland, Philadelphia, and New York as well as in border cities like Kansas City and St. Louis. These "race records" made the music more accessible than ever before.

In those days, few whites listened to the blues, preferring the danceable rhythms of 1920s jazz to the emotion and pain expressed in the moans and minor key compositions of the blues. Thus, if musicians wished to eat regularly and practice their craft, they also had to be jazz players or capable of handling whatever music was in demand. Many blues musicians like Furry Lewis played just as successfully with the traveling medicine shows as in clubs or theaters.

A Congressman Hears the Blues

Demonstrating both the power of segregation and the African-American vote around 1950 in Memphis, local Congressman George Grider with his wife and a staff member listen to Lillie Mae Glover, also known as "Ma Rainey II," perform at Sunbeam Mitchell's Club Handy on Beale Street. Normally, whites would not attend racially mixed performances on the Street. Grider did so in order to demonstrate his interest in the blues and in the welfare of blacks in Memphis. However, he did not do so in a regular public gathering. This special performance was arranged by Mitchell to include just a few representative black Memphians and the entertainers.

Whites could, and occasionally did, attend clubs and performances on Beale Street. Usually, the ones who did had no reputation to protect. In this case, the white congressman wanted to enhance his reputation with the black community, but refused to do so in a regular performance situation. Such were the customs of segregated Memphis in that era.

In other instances, composers like Handy delivered what they called "The Blues" in orchestrated form. The relatively well-educated Handy never understood the depth of delta blues even when he lived in Memphis. Because audiences for his bands were primarily white, and because whites paid better, Handy was never called upon to develop a band capable of playing the soulful blues.

The Memphis blues were, from the beginning, often "cleaned-up" written versions of delta blues. Only in the clubs on Beale, where a steady stream of blues players played when they hit town, could one find "delta blues" - even in the 1920s.

The difference is this - delta blues is spontaneous; city blues is thought out in advance and, because it has been reduced to sheet music, tends to be played the same way every time. Most delta blues players could not read music; they felt it and heard it instead. City blues players, black or white, considered it as just another type of music to put in their repertoire for the few times they played before an audience that wanted to hear "The Blues."

Musicians usually made up their delta blues as they went along. The words would be simple and straightforward. In one basic style, two lines would be worded the same but sung with increasing intensity. The third line of the verse would usually be the punch line that explained the whole verse. Rhyming was expected. If at least every other line didn't rhyme, the audience concluded the singer and songwriter needed more experience.

Another reason the delta blues did not "catch on" with whites is that the subject matter usually dealt with topics that were outside most urban white experience altogether and only blacks completely understood. The blues was always written about a problem of some sort - often caused by laws or customs set up by white society. Since whites saw little problem with restrictions that favored them, they could not fathom the depth of resentment felt by blacks so restricted.

In other cases, the problem was poverty, human nature, or the capriciousness of women (the delta blues was almost always sung by men). Whites might have some experience of this sort, but almost never of the type described by the delta blues singer.

B.B. King, an Early WDIA Blues DJ, and the Rev. A. D. "Gatemouth" Moore, WDIA's first Gospel DJ

It's impossible to know how much the decision of Bert Ferguson to team with John R. Pepper in setting up the Mid-South's first "real" black radio station affected life on Beale Street. What is clear is that it boosted Beale Street's version of the blues to new heights.

Nat D. Williams added to his history teaching responsibilities at Booker T. Washington High School by agreeing to serve as the first blues DJ on WDIA. Soon after, the Rev. Moore, a long-time popular singer and Beale Street fixture, signed on to announce the Gospel Hour shows.

B.B.'s take on life at WDIA: "The radio station reminded me of Beale Street in this respect: it was a world apart. In the middle of a strictly segregated South, WDIA was a place where blacks and whites worked together ... . I'm not saying it was perfect. Blacks couldn't be engineers; we couldn't spin the records. That was ridiculous and frustrating and made me mad." Nevertheless, B.B. saw the station as breaking new ground: "But the personalities hired by Ferguson - black deejays like Theo Wade, A.C. Williams, Hot Rod Hulbert, and Rufus Thomas - were told to be themselves. And they were."

In his book B.B. summed up the impact of WDIA: "Other stations would hire hip deejays like Dewey Phillips (Memphis' legendary deejay/promoter), white men who talked black, but blacks talking black on the air (via WDIA) to other blacks (on Beale Street and elsewhere) was something new."

Blues Into Rock

At its simplest, blues is a black music form; rock is a white music form trying to "sound black." The extent to which rock succeeded in that goal in the 1950s goes a long way toward explaining the anti-rock reaction of many horrified white parents and public officials in that decade. Robert Gordon in *It Came from Memphis* sums it up best: "Rock and roll was white rednecks trying to play black music."

Because there was at least as much black music on Beale Street and pervading the airways (thanks to WDIA) in Memphis than anywhere else in the United States, it shouldn't be too difficult to imagine why one of the birthplaces of rock was Memphis.

One of the key individuals in the development of the form was Sam Phillips, who came to Memphis in

1945 from Muscle Shoals, Alabama. Muscle Shoals today is an annexed portion of Tuscumbia, Alabama, directly across the Tennessee River from Florence, where W. C. Handy grew up more than a half century earlier.

Phillips was a white radio and recording engineer. He came to Memphis primarily because of Beale Street, blues, and his fascination with black culture. To say that those interests separated him from the bulk of white Memphians of the period is a tremendous understatement.

By 1950, Phillips was engineering recordings of black musicians at his Memphis recording studio. In Phillips' words: "I set up a studio just to make records with some of those great Negro artists." Supported financially by Memphis female radio personal-

Aretha Franklin with her Father and Memphis Pastor, C.A. Franklin, about 1970.

Aretha Franklin is rightly associated with the Motown Sound of Detroit, Michigan. But, like many others who made that record company famous, her roots are in Memphis and the South. Known as "the Queen of Soul," Aretha began her singing career in a church choir under her father's tutelage. The church-singing quality of her voice and musical selections distinguish her work from her many imitators. She occasionally performed for Sunbeam Mitchell at his Club Handy just a few blocks south of Beale Street in the 1960s.

Rufus Thomas Entertains Elvis at the 1956 WDIA Goodwill Review.

Another mainstay of the Beale Street Amateur Night shows at the Palace, Rufus Thomas supplied the comedy to accompany Nat D. Williams' venerable work as Master of Ceremonies at the events. Each year in the 1950s, WDIA radio hosted a "Goodwill Revue" showcasing the top Black performers of the Memphis area in stage performances. This particular one was memorable because a young Elvis Presley came to watch the show.

ity Marion Keisker, Phillips pursued the goal by getting acquainted with another Memphis radio disk jockey, Dewey Phillips (no relation). Sam and Dewey became lifelong friends.

Probably the most important product of their friendship was the first recording of Elvis Presley by Sam and the first broadcast of the recording by Dewey, both in 1954. Elvis' rendition of Arthur "Big Boy" Crudup's "That's All Right (Mama)" became such a hit that the not-quite-black, certainly-not-white, a little-bit-country sound became one of the earliest forms of rock 'n' roll, just then evolving in several places as a musical form.

Sam and Elvis didn't invent rock 'n' roll any more than did Bill Haley and the Comets. It is interesting, however, that both "That's All Right" and "Shake, Rattle and Roll" are essentially blues songs speeded up. Of course, they had been sped up earlier by black artists such as Crudup around Memphis and Joe Turner in Kansas City. The difference was white singers sounding just black enough, were getting airplay on white stations.

In Memphis, Dewey Phillips had been playing Beale Street music since the late 1940s on WHBQ for two hours every weeknight. Dewey didn't play just Beale Street blues, but he did play it along with a wide variety of other songs. That set

Sun Studios

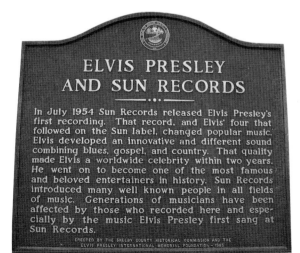

ELVIS PRESLEY AND SUN RECORDS

In July 1954 Sun Records released Elvis Presley's first recording. That record, and Elvis' four that followed on the Sun label, changed popular music. Elvis developed an innovative and different sound combining blues, gospel, and country. That quality made Elvis a worldwide celebrity within two years. He went on to become one of the most famous and beloved entertainers in history. Sun Records introduced many well known people in all fields of music. Generations of musicians have been affected by those who recorded here and especially by the music Elvis Presley first sang at Sun Records.

ERECTED BY THE SHELBY COUNTY HISTORICAL COMMISSION AND THE
ELVIS PRESLEY INTERNATIONAL MEMORIAL FOUNDATION - 1985

him apart from any other white disk jockey in Memphis or almost anywhere else in the United States in the early 1950s. White-owned stations with black deejays like WDIA in Memphis or the black-owned KPRS played music by black artists, but they appeared on the airways only in the late 1940s. Their listeners came primarily from the black communities they served.

What Sam and Dewey were doing, independently but with full knowledge of each other, was bringing about a fusing of certain aspects of race in the form of music. Interestingly, Dewey pulled this off with full support in the black community. He was as at home on Beale Street as he was anywhere else in Memphis.

Sam Phillips set up his recording studio at the end of Beale at 706 Union Avenue. Sun became known for artists like Jerry Lee Lewis, Carl Perkins and Johnny Cash.

The Sun explosion lasted just a few years. By the early 1960s, the artists all had bigger labels, more avaricious managers, and had moved into the mainstream of American music. Sam Phillips went back to his first love - radio. Dewey Phillips died in 1968 of a body worn out by too many doses of prescription muscle relaxants - a fate that would also overtake Elvis many years after.

Irving Salkey, Knox and Sam Phillips

Possibly no one else has had quite as much influence on Memphis music as Sam Phillips. Credited as the first recording engineer and record producer for Elvis Presley, Johnny Cash, Jerry Lee Lewis and Carl Perkins, Phillips passed on his love of the technical side of music to his sons, Knox and Jerry who carry on the tradition. Today, Sun Studios has established a small site in the Old Daisy Theater location on Beale between Hernando and 4th Streets. The original studio stands on Union Avenue near where Beale used to intersect with that Memphis thoroughfare.

Rhythm and Blues Blows Its Star

Although founded as a minor record label in Brunswick, Tennessee, a Memphis suburb some 20 miles from Beale Street, Stax Records had a major impact on American music in the early 1960s. Begun as Satellite Records, its first successful recording came with a small black group, the Veltones, in 1960. Actually, label owner Jim Stewart was a Brunswick banker who also played fiddle in a country band, and Satellite was started to help promote his musical hobby. Stewart's sister, Estelle Axton, worked as his bank teller by day and book-keeper for Satellite in the moonlight.

Neither Jim Stewart nor Estelle Axton had any knowledge of or interest in black musical groups. Estelle's son, Charles (nicknamed

"Packy"), took saxophone lessons from the Veltones' superb player, Gilbert Caples, whom Packy first heard playing at the Plantation Inn in wide-open West Memphis, Arkansas.

The next success for the label came from a white one-hit-wonder band called the Mar-Keys. They put together a song, "Last Night," which they parlayed into a multi-year career by exchanging players on the road just as they had in the studio making the record. The actual released version of "Last Night" involved some-thing like 25 different musicians playing at dif-ferent times in the six-piece band. Since nobody knew what the Mar-Keys actually looked like, they made up bands with different players to go play the song on weekends or on tours.

Estelle Axton, Rufus Thomas and Jim Stewart

The song's financial success brought the studio fame and fortune. It already experienced a name change. Just before releasing "Last Night," Stewart and Axton discovered that another Satellite record label already existed, so they quickly changed the name to Stax, a combination of the first two letters of their last names.

Stax went on to record mostly black artists who came to their new recording studios housed in an old theater in South Memphis. Rufus Thomas, the "world's oldest teenager," succeeded with two novelty songs reminiscent of his clowning on the Beale Street Amateur Hour shows at the Palace in the '40s and '50s. "The Funky Chicken" and "Walking the Dog" caught on just right for everybody. Other Stax artists included Otis "Sittin' on the Dock of the Bay" Redding and the integrated Booker T. & and MG's. By 1973, Stax's meteoric rise was stopped by major labels and a note that a local bank would not extend at a crucial time.

The Music Goes On

Other small studios came and went. A few, like Ardent, stayed for a long time. Yet, nothing has quite replaced the excitement created in Memphis when the blues were hot - when Sam Phillips was working magic on Union Avenue or when Stax was rolling along.

All these sounds either created or were created by Beale Street, its musicians, or its ambiance. Memphis is an independent music town, unlike its counterpart to the east, Nashville, where the big studios roll the little guys under. Ultimately, Nashville rolled Memphis music under. Still, there's always a chance that lightning might yet strike one more time in Memphis. After all, the Nashville music scene is partially populated by people who started in Memphis.

Big studios can make things happen, but they have real difficulty making something out of nothing. In Memphis, making something out of nothing seems to happen with some regularity. The latest example is none other than Beale Street herself. Counted out by everyone who knew her, lived on her, made their living by her, Beale Street is back in the late 1990s. Businesses are grossing more than ever before and the music is back home.

Two Stax Personalities: Steve Cropper and "Pop" Staples

Steve Cropper developed a good deal of the "Stax sound" as recording engineer and occasional studio guitarist. He got his start as part of the original Stax band, the Mar-Keys, and later with the Bar Kays.

The Staples Singers always proved to be one of the best Black Gospel groups anywhere. On this particular occasion, Cropper and Staples reminisced at an awards banquet.

Rum Boogie Cafe *(Bensieck Building)* 182-184 Beale

Use of this site dates to the 1880s, when Frank Bensieck built a three-story structure to house his bakery and confectionery *(candy and ice cream store)*. Bensieck and his family lived on the third floor of the business, as did many store owners on Beale.

When Frank Bensieck sold the property in 1902 and retired, the new owner, William C. Smith, tore down the bakery building and put up the present structure. For some reason, he put Bensieck's name on the plate above the corner entrance, where it remains.

The west half of the building (182 Beale) became the Beale Street Music Shop in 1927. In that era, a music shop primarily carried sheet music, although it might also have stocked phonograph records. New musical instruments could be ordered, but few were stocked because Beale Street musicians usually obtained their instruments second-hand or through pawn shops.

In the depth of the Depression in 1932, Blue Light Photography Studio took over from the music shop. It continued to photograph the more affluent of the neighborhood at this location, along with Beale Street entertainers.

Meanwhile, 184 Beale *(the Rum Boogie entrance area)* became the site of Paul's Tailoring Shop, continuing the tradition of Italian merchants on the Street. Related by marriage to the Pacinis and Barrassos, who operated the Palace and other theaters, Paul Vescova attracted many of the Beale Street entertainers who performed down in the theaters. A favorite customer who always gave good endorsements was none other than the Rev. A. D. "Gatemouth" Moore during his secular career of the the '30s and '40s

The color guard starts the procession of the Cotton Makers Jubilee Parade

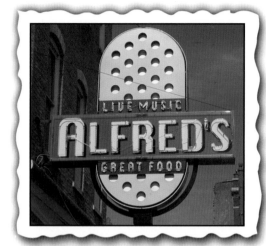

Alfred's *(Beale Avenue Market)*, 197 Beale

Constructed before 1890 for Louis Vaccaro's Saloon and Restaurant, the site of Alfred's Club at the southeast corner of Third and Beale has long served as a landmark along the Street. As with several other liquor-related businesses, this saloon disappeared around 1916 with the change in liquor laws. In its heyday, Vaccaro's offered several varieties of chili and macaroni as specialties of the house.

Briefly, in the 1920s, a newly consolidated Solvent Savings Bank operated from this location. The longest-lasting occupant, the Beale Avenue *(Food)* Market operated here from 1929 into the 1950s, when the Forty-Minute Cleaners replaced it.

Probably the building's best-known feature is the Coca-Cola advertisement on the west side. Dating from at least the 1940s, a restored two-story replica of the original billboard featuring the little man with the Coke in hand continues both to advertise and to evoke nostalgia among Baby Boomer visitors to the Street.

Beale Street Mercantile & Beale Street Tap Room both bring a slice of Americana to the street.

Memphis Music, Records, Tapes & Souvenirs (*Simon Cohen & Son Dry Goods*), 149 Beale

Though it served as the original location for A. Schwab & Sons, the Memphis Music site is better remembered for its long-time tenant, Simon Cohen and Son Dry Goods, a store handling ready-made clothing, bedding, towels and the like. Cohen's ran their operation from this store from the mid-1920s through the 1940s.

From the 1960s into the desolation of the '70s, Art Hutkin's Hardware was the building's last tenant before ultimate renovation for its current occupant. One architectural detail to note is the slightly arched wrought iron air vent grate above the top floor. Such vents are common on Beale structures, although not always as artistically done as these.

Most Beale Street buildings seem to contain relatively little architectural ornament. However, closer examination of the window openings, air vents, and doorways reveals many decorative painted wrought iron designs of delightful shapes that lend a special flavor to the buildings.

B.B. King's Blues Club (Fred L. Schwantz, succeeded by Sigmund Feder), 139-145 Beale

The current buildings housing B.B.'s place dates only from 1924. At that time, the routing of Second Street was changed, causing the original buildings occupied by Schwantz's Grocery and S. Feder Brothers Clothing to be demolished. However, both Schwantz and Feders continued their businesses in the new building.

Schwantz went out of business during the Depression. After the end of Tennessee prohibition in 1939, Dixie Liquor Store took over the site, closing in the 1960s. The final occupant before the emptying of Beale Street in the 1970s was American Loan Company's pawn shop. Feders weathered the Depression, but closed in the 1950s.

More significantly, the second floor of the structure became home to several professionals in the 1920s. Black doctors, dentists, attorneys, insurance agents, and real estate agents maintained offices there. After World War II, these tenants referred to their second-floor offices as the "Colored Business Exchange Building."

King's Palace Cafe (Epstein's Loan Office & Pawn), 162-164 Beale

King's Palace moved to this location at the time of the overall renovation in the 1980s. Constructed in 1894, the building features some distinctive wrought iron above the top story as well as around the doors and windows at ground level.

From the 1920s to the terrible times of the 1960s, it was William Epstein's Loan Office. Memphians didn't like the notion that their city abounded in pawn shops, so as early as the 1920s, many proprietors of such establishments took to calling them "loan companies."

By the late 1950s, most of Beale Street consisted of pawn shops and liquor stores, but even these establishments could not survive the emptying out of the neighborhood by desegregation and urban renewal in the late '60s and early '70s.

BEALE STREET BAPTIST CHURCH
It is considered the Mother Church of all black Baptist churches in this area. Ministers who have served this church include: Revs. Morris Henderson, Scott Key, R.N. Countee, Taylor Nightengale, P.J. Jackson, Henry Clemons, J.P. Hurt, J.C. Bowers, J. L. Lewis, B. J. Perkins, George A. Long, and James A. Jordan. Many outstanding leaders have spoken here, including President Ulysses S. Grant in 1880, U.S. Rep. Oscar DePriest in 1930, and A. Philip Randolph in 1944.
(See Other Side)
ERECTED IN 1987 BY THE BEALE STREET BAPTIST CHURCH
AND THE SHELBY COUNTY HISTORICAL COMMISSION

First Baptist Beale Street Church, 379 Beale

This venerable institution is a definite survivor as well as a cultural and religious anchor for the whole of Beale Street. Actually organized as a congregation in 1854, construction of parts of the current structure were begun in 1867. With the difficulties of race riots and cholera epidemics, as well as poor pay for congregation members, the building was not completed until 1881.

When completed, the building's towers were ornately decorated. Sadly, over time, they were damaged by weather and workmen to the extent that they were replaced by today's rather plain twin towers. Still, this is an impressive building, standing three tall stories from ground level and covering an extensive basement. The three entrances are impressively decorated with stonework.

The Daisy Theatre

As well as providing a forum for performing arts, the New Daisy Theatre offers a little twist with boxing matches on a regular basis.

SOLVENT SAVINGS BANK

The Solvent Savings Bank and Trust Company founded by Robert Church, Sr., first Negro bank established in Memphis, opened at this site, 392 Beale Street, in 1906. It survived the money panic of 1907 and became the fourth largest black bank in the nation. Robert Church, Jr. succeeded his father as president in 1912. W. C. Handy's music studio was located on the second floor in 1907.

Original Tri-State Bank (Solvent Savings Bank), 386 Beale

The Solvent Savings Bank, founded in 1906 by Robert R. Church, Sr., and more than 20 other black investors, moved into 386 Beale in 1914 after initially operating in a now-demolished building next door. A decade later, Solvent Bank, the first black-owned bank in the city and one of the first throughout the South, consolidated with another black-owned bank and moved to the building now housing Alfred's.

From 1913 to 1918, W. C. Handy operated Pace & Handy's music publishing business from a second floor office at this address. Relations with Solvent Bank were not always cordial for Handy. In 1917, after publishing "Beale Street Blues," he found himself being turned away by a bank teller when he tried to cash a $40 check. Within days of that occurrence, he received checks totaling more than $5,000 for royalties on recordings of his song. Handy recounted in later life his satisfaction at showing the largest of the checks to officers of the Solvent and then depositing them in another bank. Handy later mended fences with his landlord and redeposited the money at the Solvent, but he couldn't help gloating a bit since they had refused to cash such a small check for him just prior to the arrival of the payments.

Mostly black-owned Tri-State Bank opened its doors in December 1946 at this location. The bank has since relocated to new offices at Main and Beale, but retains ownership of the original historic property, which now serves as a private law office.

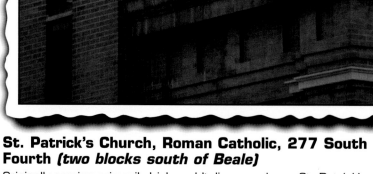

Clayborn Temple, African Methodist Episcopal Church, 294 Hernando *(two blocks south of Beale)*

Destined to play a pivotal role in the final days of Dr. Martin Luther King's leadership of the civil rights movement, Clayborn Temple, African Methodist Episcopal Church, stands sentinel today to the role that religion and dignity play in forming the Beale Street story. Many of the meetings during the sanitation strike of 1968 were held in this building. This imposing stone structure is clearly visible from the Third Street intersection with Beale as one looks toward South Memphis.

St. Patrick's Church, Roman Catholic, 277 South Fourth *(two blocks south of Beale)*

Originally serving primarily Irish and Italian members, St. Patrick's evolved into a congregation primarily serving the needs of African-American Beale Street. Just as Clayborn Temple affected life on Beale, even though it was located two blocks south, St. Patrick's played a similar role. Both churches are easily visible from Third and Beale.

Rufus Thomas
Beale Street Profile

Proclaiming himself "the World's Oldest Teenager," Rufus Thomas is one of the people who keep the original roots of Beale Street alive. At the time when he had just left his teen years, Thomas worked with Nat D. Williams to stage the Thursday Night Amateur Night competitions at the Palace Theater. Williams emceed the events while Thomas supplied the connective comedy that kept the evenings rolling along.

Thomas went on to be a major artist for Stax Records with his hits such as "Walkin' the Dog" and "Can Your Monkey Do the Dog?" His daughter, Carla, achieved a measure of fame with the same studio during the 1960s.

4E   119

RUFUS THOMAS, JR.

(Continued from other side)

He had the first hit records for both the Sun and Stax labels. As a popular personality on WDIA, he was the first disc jockey to play Elvis Presley records on a Black radio station. He was the creator of two of the biggest dance crazes of the 1960s—"The Dog" and "The Funky Chicken."

Like Williams and the Rev. "Gatemouth" Moore, Thomas also served a stint as a disk jockey on radio station WDIA. In this way, he became identified with the origins of the whole rhythm and blues movement in music. His ties to artists such as B.B. King are almost legendary.

In the late 1990s, Thomas continues to be the elder statesman of Beale Street, often presiding at special events to honor entertainers or to celebrate openings of new enterprises on the street. Probably no other living person in Memphis has been a part of the changing Beale Street scene as has Rufus Thomas.

RUFUS THOMAS BLVD

Blues City Café (Capital Loans), 138 Beale

Not surprisingly, this prime corner served as home to several saloons from its origins in the 1890s until the ouster of Mayor Crump in 1916 heralded the beginning of Tennessee Prohibition. By 1927, it was one of several different Piggly Wiggly locations (at different times) on Beale. For a few years the property owners, the Boro family, ran a sandwich shop under their own name at the location. The longest-term tenant until the present was Capital Loans, a popular pawn shop that lasted into the 1970s.

Center for Southern Folklore (Pantaze Drug Store), Hernando at Beale

Pantaze Drug Store #2 was one of the more frequently used places in this building now occupied by the Center for the Study of Southern Folklore. Abe Plough began his drug business in Memphis before 1910. In addition to selling home remedies door-to-door, he began what evolved into a chain of drug stores by the 1920s. He bought this site from George Battier, who opened the first drug store on the Street in 1896.

Plough went on to establish a huge pharmaceutical company, Plough, Inc., which marketed both prescription and non-prescription items, including St. Joseph aspirin and Coppertone suntan lotions. Abe Plough became a philanthropist, and, in 1968, he anonymously donated $60,000 to the Memphis city government to finance a pay raise for sanitation workers. The workers were on strike when Dr. Martin Luther King, Jr., was assassinated just a few blocks away.

Upstairs, Andrew "Sunbeam" Mitchell established the original Club Handy in the 1940s. Club Handy operated on the second floor, and a rooming house was available on the third floor where musicians could stay. *(This area now comprises the offices of Performa Real Estate, the managing real estate developers of today's Beale Street)*. In the 1950s, Mitchell moved the club to Georgia Street, where it evolved into Club Paradise. Almost everyone in the blues and jazz world who came through Memphis played a gig for Sunbeam Mitchell at one of these locations.

Embedded in the concrete of the sidewalk, all along Beale Street from Second to Fourth, are notes with the names of the giants of Memphis music. The Beale Street Walk of Fame Committee meets annually to choose new inductees.

Past honorees and their inscriptions include: Nat D. Williams, Historian and Amateur Night MC; the Rev. James E. Smith, the Chairman of the Beale Street Development Corporation; Harry E. Godwin, Jazz and Blues Historian; Maurice Hulbert, Sr., Dancer, also known as "the Professor of Beale Street"; Alberta Hunter,

Blues Legend; Stax Records, Home of the Memphis Sound; B.B. King, King of the Blues; Booker T. Laury; Jerry Lee Lewis, the Killer; David Porter, Soul Man; James Cotton, Superharp; The Memphis Horns: Wayne Jackson and Andrew Love; Joyce Cobb, Queen of Jazz; Memphis Slim, U.S. Ambassador of Good Will; Otis Redding, Stax Recording Legend; W. C. Handy, Father of the Blues; and the Rev. W. Herbert Brewster, "Move On Up A Little Bit Higher," Composer of Gospel Music.

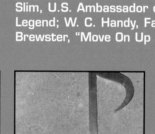
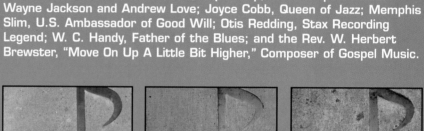

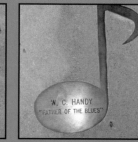
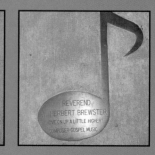

Orpheum Theater, Main at Beale

Located just west of the Historic Landmark district, the Orpheum serves as Memphis' restored grand performance theater. When the Memphis Blues Hall of Fame inducts its new members each year, the awards show and performances take place in the Orpheum. Visitors to Beale Street also have the opportunity to see traveling Broadway shows as well as some of the best area entertainers on the stage of this elegant old theater.

Air Vents: A Memphis Necessity Becomes a Beale Street Architectural Trademark

In the days before air conditioning, Memphis in the summer meant days of sweltering heat with little relief inside the buildings of Beale Street. Almost all the structures were built with sloping flat roofs, both to keep construction costs down and shed the frequent rains relatively well. Underneath the slope, contractors put in a bit of air space to cushion the top floor from the extreme temperatures that could boil up on the rooftops. In an attempt to get rid of some that heat buildup, they also built in air grates on the fronts of buildings, just under the highest point of the sloping roofs in order to let as much hot air escape as possible.

Nowadays, the air conditioning helps the customers more than the grates, but wise building owners know that even now the air flow helps reduce their electrical bills. Moreover, the grates and openings created for them actually provide a nice architectural accent on most Beale Street buildings. Next time you're on the street, look up and enjoy the practicality and the beauty of these children of necessity.

Building Decorations
Add to the Fun of Beale Street

The little things done to add delight to buildings appear in many unexpected places along Beale Street. Unlike some sections of Memphis, this was never intended to be a highly decorated area. Beale Street was intended as a working person's haven, not a shopping center for the elite.

Regardless, building contractors and architects did provide a number of little gems for our appreciation as we stroll down the street looking at the "Walk of Fame" notes or poking into shops and clubs.

Sometimes, as with the yellow painted capital on the wrought iron column, the owners or tenants of the shops have helped us see what we would otherwise miss - the little details that give character to Beale buildings.

In a few cases, plaques have been mounted. One of the most important is the one pictured for the Ernest Withers Building. This brand new structure, designed to fit in with much older buildings, houses among other shops the Withers Photographic Studio. Inside you can find living legends every day - doing what they've done for decades - recording the history of Beale Street on film.

Then too, sometimes old buildings briefly reveal something of their past uses in the signs that have faded from days gone by. The photo of the "stoves" sign retreating into the red brick illustrates a previous use for the building now open as Elvis Presley's Memphis. At one point, it served as a hardware store selling pot-bellied stoves. It all happened on Beale Street.

Symbols of Beale Street Coming Back

Beale Street in the late 1990s has literally risen from the grave. Certain building treatments give silent testament to the efforts made to save what was left of Beale and turn it into the wonderful historic entertainment district it has become. The Silky O'Sullivan patio bar is certainly one such symbol. Placed behind the shell of the old Gallina Building the grandest structure on Beale in its day - the patio serves as a place to appreciate music, the outdoors, and the human efforts to preserve and adapt for the present and future on Beale Street.

A few other buildings, like the one pictured here, demonstrate the re-enforcement necessary to hold up a building that can no longer quite do it by itself. Contractors had to sacrifice an upper floor in order to make the supports for the roof strong enough to protect the lower floors. Done as unobtrusively as possible, the effort works to help create the overall message that, indeed, Beale Street Is Back! The Music Is Back!

Silky O'Sullivan's Patio

Once covered by the grandest building on Beale Street—the Gallina Hotel and Bar, this open patio dining, drinking and entertainment area now stands behind all that is left of the landmark structure. So badly damaged that the building itself could not be salvaged, and sitting right on the Gayoso Bayou so that no new structure could replace it, the Gallina facade continues to front Beale while setting off this marvelous party area from the street itself. The whole setting is unduplicated anywhere in Memphis or the South.

Silky O'Sullivan's Facade and Gallina Building

A massive amount of construction and reconstruction was necessary to create the current Beale Street environment. Around 1980, all that stood on the site that now houses Silky O'Sullivan's nightclub was the facade. Ironically, in contrast, the entire Gallina Building structure stood at that site. During the construction of the 1980s, the entire Silky O'Sullivan building behind the two-story front was rebuilt and decorated to look like it had been there for 100 years. The Gallina Building proved to be unsound and was razed, except for the facade. Because the building stood on what was once the Gayoso Bayou, city building codes prevented any substantial new construction of the historic site. Hence, the facade was shored up with steel I-beams and the area behind it was turned into an open-air bar and entertainment-area as part of the Silky O'Sullivan operation next door.

Sale Day at A. Schwab's, 1920s

The everyday prices of dry goods and other items at A. Schwab's were normally quite reasonable, but when sales were announced, women of the Beale Street community gathered early to take advantage of the discounts. This bonnet-wearing crowd clearly planned to get there first for the best bargains. Note that at that time, Schwab's occupied only one storefront, compared to their current two-storefront operation. The lettering on the sign overhead is instantly recognizable, whether the date is 1927 or 1997.

Drawing considerably less attention, the Piggly Wiggly next door stood ready to offer the ladies groceries, canned goods, and dried foods at competitive prices. Originating in Memphis in 1917, just prior to World War I, the Piggly Wiggly chain pioneered the concept of self-service grocery stores. Before the Piggly Wiggly, grocery stores had clerks select the products requested by patrons standing at a counter. The new style of advertising products by their packaging made such stores as Piggly Wiggly possible.

Beale Street View from Fourth Street Looking West, 1940s

This is the section of the Street where some of the greatest changes have occurred. Almost all the buildings on the left side have been replaced with appropriately styled new structures (including the Ernest Withers Building). The facade of the Old Daisy Theater remains on the left, but is almost invisible here. On the right, almost the only remaining unaltered structure is the New Daisy Theater (the marquee extends over sidewalk on right).

These streetcar tracks running double down the middle of Beale Street make a striking image. Like most U.S. cities, Memphis phased out electric streetcars in the 1950s. Also unusual is the horse-drawn wagon in the right-hand lane. Hucksters still plied Beale Street, selling fresh produce and other items as late as the post-World War II era. The numbers of automobiles lining the street in parallel parking slots indicates that this was a prosperous era, probably during World War II.

Greener's Department Store, Hernando and Beale, 1940s

One of the best-known of all the Beale Street clothing stores during the first half of the 20th century, Greener's ultimately became Harris's and then closed its doors. The building stood in the same half block as the Palace and New Daisy Theaters as well as the current Willie Mitchell's.

Greener's offered clothing and other dry goods to the Beale Street community at competitive prices and in styles that the neighborhood appreciated. More than one blues singer hit the road with clothes purchased within these walls. Its location opposite Handy Park across Hernando made it a popular rendezvous point for area residents.

Born and raised in Memphis and educated at Manassas High School, Ernest Withers has worked on the Beale Street beat for more than 50 years. As a young married man, he joined 9 other young black men in 1948 to train to become the first uniformed black policemen in Memphis since the 1880s.

Boss Crump was waning in power - not in Memphis elections, but no longer could he always get his man elected in state-wide polls. To shore up his influence at home, he allowed the city government to do something he had long resisted - put uniformed black policemen on the street. As Withers relates, in the beginning this was only a partial victory. The 10 newly minted uniformed cops hit the streets only on the "graveyard shift" (11 p.m. to 7 a.m.) and then only in the Beale Street section and in other black communities such as Orange Mound. It was a small beginning for Memphis and, as we know now, not nearly enough to account for all the years E. H. Crump held to his segregationist, patronizing policies toward half the city's population. Ernest Withers did not stay a policeman for long. That familiar Beale Street regular, Nat D. Williams, encouraged him to submit photos to the newspapers for which Nat D. wrote columns. Nat D. recognized Ernest Withers' ability to visualize a picture, and he encouraged the young policeman to pursue his dream. By 1950, Ernest Withers was doing just that.

Sometimes his photography shop was in places like the second floor of the Palace Theater. In 1968, as in most of the years to the present, you entered the Withers Photography Studio directly off Beale Street. Now there's even an Ernest Withers Building in the 400 block of Beale.

Withers has been more than just a Memphis photographer. With a little nudge from Nat D., he went to Little Rock in 1956 to visually document the desegregation of Central High School. When Emmitt Till was lynched for smiling at a white girl in Mississippi in the early 1960s, Ernest photographed evidence of the outrage. The Medgar Evers murder, the last days of Dr. Martin Luther King, the evidences of Memphis' segregationist policies - all became fodder for Ernest Withers' photographic mill.

Now, on Beale Street, there is a note placed in the sidewalk indicating Nat D. Williams as "historian." Just down the block there's the plaque on the building saying "The Ernest Withers Building." Time has come full circle.

Young Ernest Withers in Front of His Beale Street Photography Studio, early 1950s.

Following a brief stint as one of Memphis' first Black uniformed police-men, Withers followed the advice of Nat D. Williams and set up his own photography business. In those days most of the jobs revolved around social functions and church gatherings where people might "want their picture taken." Ernest Withers has become justly famous for many of the documentary photographs he has taken of events dur-ing the civil rights movement, but the financial success of his business still depends on people wanting "their picture taken."

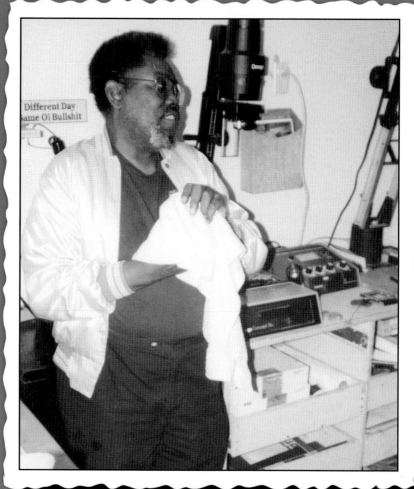

Ernest Withers' "Right-Hand Man," Richard Jones

For almost thirty years, Mr. Withers has shared the responsibil-ities of his photography work with another Memphis native. Richard Jones attributes his longevity to flexibility and his ability to get along with most folks. Mr. Jones has seen and recorded on film a large number of significant Beale Street events over his own tenure as a Beale Street photographer.

The First Uniformed Black Policemen in Memphis (Ernest Withers, second from right), 1948

For many years in the 20th century, Memphis had black policemen, but they were always designated as detectives and wore plain clothes. Their mission was to investigate crime in the black community around Beale Street. While it might seem as though this was an advancement for black policemen to be plain-clothes detectives, the reality was that the police department did not really want people - black or white - to know that there were any black policemen at all.

Over many decades, leaders in the Memphis black community tried to get members of their race in uniform. Finally, in 1948, after Memphis political boss E. H. Crump suffered a political defeat, the city hired and trained 10 black policemen to patrol the area in uniform. Ernest Withers had not yet started his long career in photography, so he applied for one of the first openings. He states that, initially, all the policemen pictured here patrolled Beale Street and environs only during the graveyard shift (11 p.m. to 7 a.m.). Over time, their hours were adjusted and integrated patrols ultimately became common by the 1970s.

Carter Ryan's Market [now Alfred's], 1950

This prime location at the intersection of 3rd Street and Beale has served the community in many capacities. One of the longest tenants was this grocery store. Officially called "Carter Ryan's Beale Avenue Market," the name reflects the city of Memphis's attempt to convert Beale to an "avenue" rather than a street. For local residents, the seemingly high sounding title "avenue" never caught on. It just didn't sound right to talk about "The Beale Avenue Blues." Beale Street has always been Beale Street, no matter what Boss Crump or anybody else said!

Looking east from Hernando on Beale, 1960s.
Some of the significant changes in buildings and locations on the east end of Beale Street become apparent in this Ernest Withers photo. Beale Street was already somewhat in decline when this photo was taken around 1960, but several buildings existed on both sides of the street which were gone before the current renovation of the street got underway in the late 1980s.

The Gallina Building *[Silky O'Sullivan's Patio]*, **1970s**

Already largely closed up, the Gallina building still dominated the block on Beale between 2nd and 3rd Streets. Physically, it was the most imposing structure in the Historic District which runs from 2nd to 4th along Beale Street. The building served as the Gallina Hotel and Saloon from the 1890s to the onset of Tennessee's prohibition against alcohol in 1909.

After the Palace was Gone, 1970s

The Palace Theater served as one of the great performing houses for Black Vaudeville in the 1920s and '30s. Later it became home to the Beale Street Amateur Night competitions conducted by Nat D. Williams. Torn down in the early 1970s, the Palace came to symbolize the futility of many of the early efforts to "save" Beale Street. By the time John Elkington and Performa took over the ultimately successful effort in the late 1980s, the Palace was sadly just a memory.

THE HUNT-PHELAN HOME

DURING THE CIVIL WAR, THE HOUSE WAS COMMANDEERED BY GENERAL ULYSSES GRANT AS HIS MEMPHIS HEADQUARTERS; JEFFERSON DAVIS, PRESIDENT OF THE CONFEDERACY, AND A FRIEND OF THE HUNT FAMILY, ALSO SPENT TIME IN THE HOUSE. LATER, IT WAS USED AS A FEDERAL HOSPITAL. DURING RECONSTRUCTION, IT SERVED AS AN OFFICE OF THE FREEDMAN'S BUREAU, AND A SCHOOL FOR FORMER SLAVES WAS ON THE GROUNDS.

CONSTRUCTION OF THE HOUSE STARTED IN 1828 AND WAS COMPLETED IN 1832. IT HAS BEEN OWNED BY MEMBERS OF THE SAME FAMILY TO THE PRESENT.

THE NATIONAL SOCIETY OF THE COLONIAL DAMES OF AMERICA IN THE STATE OF TENNESSEE-MEMPHIS COMMITTEE 1996

The Hunt-Phelan Home

Located just east of Danny Thomas Boulevard on Beale Street, this is the last of the old Beale Street mansions. During the period from 1840-1860, much of the length of Beale Street was lined by large houses built for wealthy White families. The Hunt-Phelan Home was constructed between 1828 and 1832. During the Civil War, Union General Grant took over the house and grounds for his Memphis headquarters. At a different time during the war, Confederate President Jefferson Davis stayed with the Hunt family in the house. Still later it was used as a Union hospital. It remained under one family ownership until placed under foundation ownership in the 1990s and converted to a house museum.

The Volunteer Ticket Campaign, 1958.

Even four years after the death of Boss Ed Crump, the city government of Memphis continued to be dominated by White politicians. What was worse, the post-Crump Democrats seemed even less interested in the needs of the Black community and Beale Street than the old boss had been in his last years.

Russell Sugarmon, Benjamin Hooks, Rev. Love, and C.H. Williams all attempted to get the form of Memphis city government changed from the commission style with all commissioners elected at large to designated districts for city council members. The immediate campaign did not succeed, but it set in motion forces which did gain a change of governmental form in the 1960s.

"Don't Buy Gas Where You Can't Use the Restroom"

As early as 1952, civil rights organizers in the Beale Street Black community attempted to rally support for their cause. The reference in the bumper sticker alluded to the fact that most "modern" gasoline filling stations had either two restrooms ["Men" & "Women"] which Blacks were not allowed to use, or if they had a "Colored" rest room, it was for the use of men and women alike. The appeal is to get Blacks to boycott either practice.

The Day After the Beale Street March, March 1968

Dr. Martin Luther King's last public march ended in a riot with young men breaking windows and looting stores rather than following Dr. Martin Luther King and others to City Hall. The remnants of the march are apparent in the presence of the National Guard troops and tanks on Beale Street. The large dark brick building in the center was replaced in the 1970s by the Memphis Light Gas and Water building.

The Post-Assassination March for the Sanitation Workers, April 8, 1968

Partly to prove that a successful civil rights march was still possible even after the killing of Dr. King, Memphis organizers led this group along Main Street. Here at the corner of 2nd and Beale they looked carefully about them in order to avoid the possibility of similar events less than two weeks before.

Party Time at Red Johnny's

During the years of "BYOB" (1939-1980), when liquor was only available in package form in Tennessee, proprietor Brown sold "set-ups" of soft drinks to patrons using the party room. Note the 7-Up bottles on the table along with the larger bottles of alcohol. One brand of liquor available during the heyday of the "Brown Bomber," heavyweight champion Joe Louis, carried the name of the famous boxer. These well-dressed citizens of the Beale Street neighborhood have gathered at Red Johnny's for a special occasion. The lack of air conditioning was only partly alleviated by the large floor fan in the background. These "raw blues joints" also catered to a more upscale crowd, since places for community gathering were important to the maintenance of the spirit of Beale Street at all levels of black Memphis society.

Curry's Old Tropicana Club, North Memphis

Not all Memphis night life in the black community occurred on Beale Street - it only seemed that way at the time. Johnny Curry started the Tropicana in the 1950s as a night club where you could get a set-up and a good cigar as well as dance the night away. Here the serving crew and manager are ready to open for a full night's business.

North Memphis was home to the city's other black high school, Manassas High. Booker T. Washington, established in the 1920s, was the city's oldest black high school.

W.C. Handy Statue in Handy Park

The city of Memphis established W.C. Handy Park in 1938 as the first monument to an African American in the city. It was somewhat controversial at the time because Handy was still living. Previously, the site housed an old market building which had fallen into disrepair. After the dedication, the city commissioned this statue to be sculpted and placed in the park as a reminder of the man from Beale Street who became "father of the blues."

W. C. Handy lived in Memphis from the 1890s through 1915. When the state government removed Boss Crump as mayor in 1915, it paved the way for the first real enforcement of Tennessee's Prohibition law, which had been enacted in 1909. The closing down, at least temporarily, of Beale Street's saloons and beer joints occasioned both Handy's composition of the "Beale Street Blues" and his move to New York City. Beginning in 1939, he returned to Memphis each year for the high school Blues Bowl.

W.C. Handy Appearance at a "Blues Bowl" celebration. Early 1950s

Here the grand old Bluesmaster shakes hands with Lucy Campbell of Memphis as Maurice "Hot Rod" Hulbert looks on. Hulbert served as a DJ on WDIA along with Nat D. Williams, B.B. King, and others during the early days of that pioneering radio station.

The "Blues Bowl" games featured the football teams of Booker T. Washington and Manassas High Schools. Handy made it a point to return to Memphis for the parade and game held in his honor each year beginning in 1939. The "father of the blues" lived and worked in New York City from 1916 until his death in the late 1950s.

Commissioner Jones and Lt. George W. Lee of the Elks ride with W. C. Handy at a "Blues Bowl" game in the 1940s

The Black Elks formed an important institution in the Beale Street community. Not only did their clubhouse serve as the location for many social gatherings, the fraternal organization's leadership provided direction for the entire community. Lt. Lee became the Republican political leader of Beale Street and as late as 1960 he could bring together large crowds to hear Jackie Robinson endorse Richard Nixon in Church Auditorium or to see the candidate himself visit Handy Park.

This parade with the three men featured occurred in either 1940 or 1941 at the Blues Bowl football game played between Booker T. Washington High School and Manassas High School, the two black secondary schools in the city.

Herman Rankin and His Combo in Handy Park

His day job was as band-master at one of the Memphis high schools. At night, however, Herman Rankin supplemented his small teacher's salary by leading a jazz and blues combo that played at parties and in an occasional concert. This particular instance shows the group in concert at old handy Park. By the 1990s, the Handy statue was moved closer to Beale Street and the restoom building in the background was removed.

B.B. King with the Bill Harvey Band, 1953

In the early 1950s, B.B. King found himself able to record hit music and to be a headliner, at least with small bands. The problem was that his tour manager put together different bands for almost every one-night stand. Sometimes the back-up was great; more frequently, it was lousy. B.B. decided that the problem was his own lack of control over his tour and band.

In Memphis, B.B. admired Bill Harvey, a Beale Street regular. Harvey had a talent for putting together good bands in short order. He knew everybody in the Memphis and Beale Street music scene, and he worked out arrangements that took advantage of each player's strengths while covering up their weaknesses.

Bill put B.B. in touch with the Buffalo Booking Agency out of Houston, which helped King get a better sense of direction for his career. Of this Ernest Withers picture, B.B. said in his recent autobiography, *Blues All Around Me*, "I thought my Bermuda shorts were Esquire-ish." Whatever they were, this is a B.B. King who sang and played the blues, but had clearly left the Delta.

Riley "B.B." King and His Wife, Martha, 1942.

B.B. and Martha married in 1942 in the courthouse at Indianola, Mississippi. They met while B.B. was driving a tractor and Martha picked cotton in the Delta country of Sunflower County. It was an eight-year marriage full of ups and downs.

In 1946, Riley made his first trip to Memphis partly to visit his cousin, bluesman "Bukka" White. The trip gave B.B. his first taste of Beale Street. B.B. says, "I found Beale Street to be a city unto itself. It was exciting seeing so many people crowded on the streets. So much activity, so much life, so many sounds. The hot part of Beale Street was only four blocks long, snuggled behind downtown and the famous Hotel Peabody, where the rich businessmen stayed and plotted their fortunes. Beale Street did look like heaven to me." Without a doubt, the young B.B. never in the world imagined that one day he would have his own club along those four blocks of heaven.

The Pride of Beale Street Hits the Road in His First Bus, 1955

This picture of B.B. Kings's first band was taken next to King's Palace Café one cloudy morning in 1955. Together with a Beale Street CPA named Jessee Turner, B.B. got a bank loan to buy and refurbish the bus. Cato Walker, brother to B.B.'s road manager James Walker, was a first-rate mechanic who kept the big Aero bus humming … most of the time.

This first B.B. King band included people who worked with B.B. for years afterwards. Most were Beale Streeters at the time. Two women graced the group. Benita Cole was the "girl singer," but Evelyn "Mama Nuts" Young was the band's lead saxophonist. Earl Forest and Ted Curry played drums. Millard "Mother" Lee did the piano work. Floyd Newman, Richard "Dickie Boy" Lillie, and Lawrence Burdine all backed Mama Nuts on the saxophones. Kenny Sands and Calvin Owens did the trumpet lines while Jerry Smith played bass. It was quite a group.

B.B. King Celebrates Rufus Thomas's Birthday

Two of the longtime mainstays of life on Beale Street recently celebrated Thomas's birthday. B.B. King and Rufus Thomas met when the latter served as "clown-in-residence" for Beale Street's Amateur Nights in the 1940s. B.B. came along as a contestant. Although King seldom won the competition, Thomas kept letting him in, giving the young blues singer the exposure and confidence that helped to build his fabulous career.

B.B. King and Elvis at the WDIA Good Will Revue, December 7, 1956

WDIA began broadcasting as a rhythm and blues/gospel station in 1949, and in the early '50s, began an annual benefit concert for "needy Negro children" in Ellis Auditorium, downtown Memphis. The show featured the station's personalities and Rufus Thomas as "Chief Rockin' Horse," while Nat D. Williams was on hand as himself to crown the station's queen, "Miss 1070" (WDIA's number on the AM dial).

Show headliners included Ray Charles, B.B. King (who worked his way up to part-time disc jockey on WDIA before hitting the big time), the Magnificents and the Moonglows. Through a series of personal contacts, Elvis was invited simply to make an appearance. Now under the management of Col. Tom Parker, Presley readily agreed to appear, but declined to perform, watching the entire show from the wings.

At the conclusion of the show, Thomas invited him to come out and say a few words. Presley responded with a "How you doing?" The crowd called out for him to do something, so he gave a little hip shake. The entirely black audience, particularly the teenage girls went wild.

Black newspapers commented afterwards how polite Presley had been. The Tri-State Defender indicated that "Presley was heard telling King, 'Thanks, man, for the early lessons you gave me.'"

Rufus Thomas' daughter, Carla, said that Elvis stayed and talked with performers and others backstage until the auditorium manager told them it was time to go. "He stayed that long, and we were just having a lot of fun. I remember that Elvis."

Elvis Presley with Clarence Earl and Perry Withers, 1956

On a different night, but clearly at about the same time as the Good Will Revue, photographer Ernest Withers took this picture of two of his six sons with Presley. Afterwards, Withers asked the boys what Elvis said to them after the photo was taken. They replied, "Nothing much, he just invited us to come visit him at his house."

With all the hype and noise of Elvis's later career, it is easy to forget the almost shy, quite open Elvis of the early years. His lack of racial prejudice in a town in which the disease ran rampant helped set the stage for the future openness of all of rock 'n' roll without regard to race.

Elvis Presley and Brooke Benton, 1956

On the same night he snapped the picture of his sons with Elvis, Withers photographed Elvis backstage with an early R & B singer, Brooke Benton, who made the crossover to smooth rock. Once again, the connection between the blues and rock becomes clear in the Beale Street music story.

B. B. King, Muddy Waters, Howlin Wolf and Big Joe Turner

Three young ball players get an opportunity to meet some blues legends including B. B. King, Howlin Wolf, Muddy Waters and Big Joe Turner.

Muddy Waters

Muddy Waters wows the audience.

Albert King

Albert King celebrates his birthday at the Blues City Cafe.

Sunbeam Mitchell in Front of his Club Paradise

Located south of Beale Street, Club Paradise served as a major venue for acts that also performed in some clubs on the street from the 1940s into the 1970s. Mitchell started his music promotion work in the building now occupied by the Center for Southern Folklore at Hernando and Beale. His first Club Handy [later renamed Club Paradise] operated on the second floor of that structure. In the later Beale Street years, Mitchell performed the promotional duties that kept much of the Beale Street sound alive.

Ike and Tina Turner at Sunbeam Mitchell's Paradise Club, 1960s

Ike and Tina Turner brought their musical revue to town for recording and performing sessions. As always, Sunbeam Mitchell recognized hot talent when he saw it and booked them into his Paradise Club as often as possible. During these early days, Ike Turner was the equal of anyone in developing a marketable sound. While their marriage ended in a divorce resulting from well-publicized abuse, Ike and Tina Turner formed a very successful combination for a period in Memphis music history.

Members of the Bobby Blue Bland Band, 1970s

Shown in performance at Mitchell's Club Paradise, the Bobby Blue Bland Band became one of the premier back-up groups in Beale Street musical history. Using the eletric guitar and horns such as the saxophone, they transformed blues into the kind of entertainment that would ultimately win back listeners who had gone after other sounds. Bland and B.B. King still function as two of the major blues performers in the United States in the late 1990s.

Little Laura Dukes & Son Just Perform with Combo at Liberty Bowl, early 1970s.

Two legendary Blues performers, Just and Dukes, combine their talents with a Memphis combo group to enliven the festivities at one of Memphis' premier events—the Liberty Bowl. Above, the same performers add their distinctive sounds to those of a Memphis High School in an indoor performance. By the 1970s Memphis began fully to include its Blues heritage in its public image.

Lillie Mae Glover Holds Forth, about 1980

Lillie Mae Glover lived near and entertained on Beale Street over several decades. Sometimes billed as "Ma Rainey II," Glover settled in Memphis in the 1920s and continued to call it home until her death in 1985. In an interview conducted not long before her passing, Glover described her heritage with the blues. "All my people were church people, understand. My father was a pastor. See, the blues was borned in me, but my people never sung the blues in their life. That's the worst in the world to them, the blues was. But they couldn't get those blues out of me."

There was, indeed, a chasm between blues singers and many church-going people in Memphis' black community. The blues were usually sung in a "juke joint" in the rural areas or in a bar in the city. God-fearing people did not publicly go to those places. In spite of this, many church-going people felt the intensity of the blues and its rhythms. Hence, music in the many black churches tended to be either deeply sorrowful or unusually boisterous. Black gospel music is a variation of the blues with sacred texts and meanings.

Lillie Mae Glover understood all this implicitly, but could never convince her family that what she sang was not that different from what they sang at church. She described another instance in her youth when she first started singing. "We were living in Nashville, Tennessee, and they had a carnival show that came there. You could sing the blues for a prize. My people (family) didn't allow me out, understand, but I slipped up there with another girl and slipped upon the stage and I sang the blues. Someone went home and got my people. They like to kill me." (Beale Black and Blue, p. 146)

The Bob Tally Combo

Keyboard artist Bob Tally gathered this collection of musicians together in the 1970s to perform in a number of nightspots. In addition to Tally at left, Bernard Clark served as drummer, Robert "Fat Sonny" Williamson held forth on the saxophone, and Wilbert Steinberg played guitar for the group.

The Albert King Funeral Procession on Beale Street

Although a frequent custom in New Orleans, the idea of a musical parade serving as funeral procession rarely occurs in Memphis. In a great tribute to their friend and fellow bluesman, this assemblage of performers broke Memphis tradition by marching up Beale Street, past B.B. King's Club, and on to the riverfront in the early 1990s.

Sylvester "Big Lucky" Carter

Sylvester Carter, Beale Street guitarist and WDIA personality, still plays at clubs and special events in the Memphis area. Though he learned to play on an acoustic guitar in the country, Carter adapted to the times as necessary. Because an electric guitar could make so many more sounds, a musician with a Fender or Gibson became a whole band.

Herman Green and Calvin Newborn Perform Live, 1980s

A master of the tenor saxophone, Herman Green held forth in this concert photo. He was backed by one of the best post-World War II guitarists in the business, Calvin Newborn, son of Phineas.

Phineas Newborn at the Piano

One of the great Blues-Jazz pianists of the Memphis region, Phineas Newborn began his career playing at the Plantation Inn in West Memphis, Arkansas just across the Mississippi River from downtown Memphis and Beale Street.

Trumpeteer Luther Steinberg Makes Nat D. Williams Laugh, early 1970s

In this relaxed scene following a concert by Steinberg, the performer met Master of Ceremonies Nat D. Williams in the backstage area.

Being a Master of Ceremonies was nothing new to Williams. Throughout the 1940s and '50s he emceed the Beale Street Amateur Night competitions at the old Palace Theater. Williams was a man for all seasons. His musical interests led him to become the first Black disk jockey at WDIA in the late 1940s while his literary abilities contributed a constant stream of columns to the old Memphis newspaper, *The Globe*. His day job had him teaching American History to high school juniors at Booker T. Washington High School, Memphis' oldest black high school.

His memory is preserved on Beale Street in the form of one of the notes embedded in the sidewalk commemorating Beale Street musicians and leaders. His inscription includes his name and the description, "Historian."

There's nothing quite like the splash of color that spreads over nighttime crowds along Beale Street. The light casts its wondrous glow; blues and rock music fill the air; it's time to celebrate on a Beale Street Saturday night!

As the sun sets on Beale Street the night comes alive with hot blues acts like Sherman Robertson at B. B. King's (left), Preston Shannon at the Band Box (right) and The Boogie Blues Band at The Rum Boogie Cafe (large photo).

Aspiring Musician Waits His Turn to Play at an Impromptu Concert in Handy Park

Will Memphis Music ever die? Not if there are musicians like this gentleman ready to step forward and take up the mantle. Whether it's the Blues, Rock, or something in between, Memphis and its territories have always produced the players who make the music machine go. Handy Park serves as just the sort of venue needed by these people wishing to find stardom.

Park Dancing on Beale Street

Handy Park at Beale and Hernando is more than just a place to lounge while waiting for the clubs to open. Particularly during festival times, it becomes the great outdoor performing and enjoyment spot. Bands play on, individual artists cater to smaller groups clustered about, and young and old alike cannot resist the possibilities for getting up and dancing to the music. It's contagious!

Street Performers on Beale Street

Just when you think you've seen all the varieties of entertainment possible, street performers on Beale Street prove you wrong. Literally dancing for their supper, these agile break dancers also perform a variety of almost gymnastic feats to the delight of the crowds.

The Memphis Horns Perform in Handy Park

One of the better known ensembles of studio musicians in the United States, the Memphis Horns provide pizazz to any gathering. This particular appearance on Beale Street demonstrated their versatility as well as the various uses Handy Park provides along the street. Often the scene of impromptu concerts by mostly unknown musicians, it can also become the setting for outstanding professional groups as well.

Jason D. Williams Does a Handstand on his Piano on Beale Street

One of the premier entertainers on Beale Street is Jason D. Williams. He uses hands, feet, boots, and various other portions of his anatomy to rock his audience.

Leon Russell Strolls on Beale Street

You never know who you'll meet on this famous thoroughfare. In this case, it was longtime performer Leon Russell as only he could be. Beale Street has always been a place where you could meet interesting people. In the old days, a lot of Memphis was afraid to come down to Beale Street, but those days are gone. It's a wonderful blend of all the shades of people and lifestyles that make up modern Memphis and modern America.

King Daddy, One of the Many Blues Performers on Beale Street.

The Blues is a musical style that is both simple and complllicated. The lyrics are repetitive, but the chords and "blue" notes require careful fingering on guitars and horns. Few white performers have ever really developed an authentic blues style. One who has is a regular fixture at Alfred's [in front of which he is pictured here]. Known as King Daddy, he specializes in the blues as styled by Muddy Waters who grew up less than 50 miles south of Memphis in northern Mississippi.

The New Elvis Statue

Unveiled as a part of the opening of Elvis Presley's Memphis club, this statue is located across the street on the grounds of the Memphis municipal utilities building at 2nd & Beale. There has long been a statue of Elvis at this location on the street, but the old one had been marred by weather and vandals. The new bronze figure illustrates a young Elvis as he might have looked strolling by on these very blocks of Beale Street in the early 1950s.

During music festival periods, and there are many throughout the year in Memphis and along Beale Street, performers and groups take to stages in Handy Park to play their music and entertain the milling crowds. While the quality of the music may vary, the variety and vitality these park and street performers bring to the party atmosphere of the festivals is essential.

The festival crowds grow even larger and more enthusiastic for the "name" acts that perform on the various stages. "Seating" becomes "standing room." The amplified sounds of traditional blues players, varieties of rock artists, folk and gospel acts all hold forth to move the audience to full participation with shouts, sing-alongs, and "swaying to the music." There seems to be a contest between the musicians and the crowd as to which does more to energize the other. Certainly, if a particular performer does not create crowd involvement, the numbers dwindle rapidly as people seek the excitement of a band that's really with it on a hot afternoon like this.

The Tracy Nelson group has no difficulty energizing a recent Beale Street Blues International Music Festival crowd. Framed by the high levee protecting the city from Mississippi floods, along with the beauty of the river herself rolling down toward New Orleans and the Gulf of Mexico, both band and crowd sense the special quality of the moment. It is a setting not duplicated by any other blues or jazz festival in the entire country. Blues sung at its fount, a park venue bordered by the greatest river on the continent, and gorgeous spring days that enliven everyone in sight - all these elements are to be found at "Memphis in May."

Crowd scene at the Beale Street Festival

Expect lots of people at the Beale Street International Musical Festival in Tom Lee Park every May. Most are there for the music and the sun like this group. Others come for the sheer delight of catching a few rays while sampling the music in between. Then, there are the people watchers who delight in observing the variety of humanity which comes to enjoy these rare days in May every year. Whatever the reason for coming, Memphis in May on Beale Street is the place to be!

A. Schwab — the Survivor

When John Elkington and the Performa group took over Beale Street redevelopment in 1982, only two businesses were still in existence. Abe Schwab and his sons, together with Ernest Withers' photography studio, comprise the "old timers" on the Street.

The A. Schwab Department Store had already persisted in the same location on Beale Street since the close of Reconstruction following the Civil War (1876). Schwab's is a 19th century department store that has never modernized. Unvarnished pine floors, here and there splintered by use, create just the right atmosphere for sorting through the piles of clothing, curios, and assorted stuff that are regularly heaped on rectangular "display islands." There is a little museum on the "mezzanine" - if such a fancy word can be used for the enlarged stair landing. It features memorabilia from the last 120 years or so.

Abe Schwab is the third generation of his family to preside over this retail

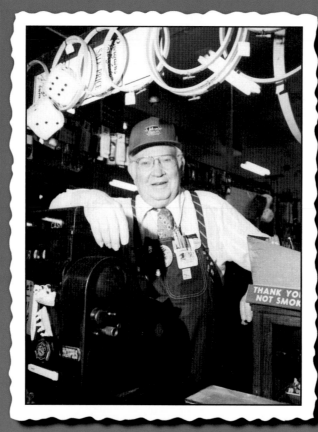

establishment, and his sons, who work with him, fully intend to carry on the tradition. Schwab says the biggest change for him in today's Beale Street is in the number of tourists who flock to his store - as if drawn by the healthy assortment of refrigerator magnets he stocks. But maybe it's the complete sets of Fiesta ware - that post-depression pottery that became the "everyday dishes" for so many families across middle America in the 1950s.

Whatever the market will bear (and buy), you'll probably find a little of it in Schwab's. But then, that observation is unnecessary when you see the store's slogan: "If you can't find it at Schwab's, you probably don't need it."

Through years of blues joints, gambling dens, church parades, pawn shops, racial unrest, and now a tourist attraction, Schwab's has witnessed it all on Beale Street. If Robert R. Church, Sr., could somehow now revisit the store he knew at the turn of the century, he'd probably still recognize the place.

Schwab's by Day

The familiar red, white and blue bunting is up at Schwab's. That means a sale is in progress. Visitors flock inside, leaving the street briefly empty of passers-by. The action is all on the inside. Schwab's has been conducting sales since it opened on Beale in the 1870s. No other store in Memphis or the Mid-South offers quite the experience available every day in this venerable establishment.

Elvis Presley's Memphis

One of the newest attractions along Beale Street, Elvis Presley's Memphis provides a bit of Graceland right on this historic street. Elvis certainly visited Beale Street in his early days. Sometimes he would visit the clubs accompanying his friend, disk jockey Dewey Phillips. Other times he bought guitars or outfits in the pawn shops and clothing stores along Beale Street in the 1950s.

Beale Street merchants offer an array of shopping experiences.

Beale Street Mercantile, The Band Box and Blues City Cafe are just a few of the stops tourists from all over the world make on their journey to Beale Street.

The Black Diamond, Memphis Music and B.B. King's light up the sidewalk at dusk.

Willie Mitchell's Blues Club

Willie Mitchell's Rhythm and Blues Club at 326 Beale Street, plays host to many regional as well as national blues acts.

Strange Cargo on Beale Street

Powered by its cartoon advertisement in which a young lady says to her man, "I feel strange; must be the cargo," this intriguing boutique offers Beale Street souvenirs and so much more. By now almost an institution on the street, Strange Cargo specializes in the unique as well as the mundane. A stop here is a must.

The Willis Gallery (Formerly Gestine's) 156 Beale

Since much of the Beale Street scene emanates from the clubs and cafes, other small businesses are most welcome for the variety they provide. The Willis Gallery specializes in art that represents or interprets African American life, the Beale Street traditions, and the best in modern art the world over.

Sitting in Front of Silky's

The steel supports for the Gallina Building that fronts Silky O'Sullivan's Patio are set into concrete that forms a nice place to sit on Beale Street during a hot Festival afternoon. This was one of those accidental results of construction done for other purposes that help to make certain places unique. The designers did not have the comfort of Beale Street visitors in mind so much as they were concerned for the safety when the steel girders went up. Creative party-goers on the street quickly adapted the concrete base for their own lounging area. It's another distinctive aspect to the whole of Beale Street.

Silky O'Sullivans
Dualing piano players Danny and Joe get the crowd involved at Silky O'Sullivans.

Beale Street Welcomes the Hard Rock Cafe

Another new attraction on Beale Street is located just across from Handy Park. The Hard Rock Cafe is a premier attraction wherever it chooses to place a restaurant. Its place as a centerpiece of the new Beale Street is assured.

Reba Russell and her band perform at the Hard Rock Cafe.

Lt. George W. Lee
Beale Street Profile

Beale Street's Political Leader, Lt. George W. Lee

The military title resulted from World War I service where Lee became one of a handful of the first commissioned Black officers in United States Army history. Born and educated in Mississippi, Lee returned after the War and settled in Memphis. He aligned himself politically with Robert R. Church, the staunchly Republican financial benefactor of Beale Street. In national elections, the two led the Beale Street community to vote Republican even through the Great Depression.

After Church moved to Chicago in the late '30s, Lee continued his leadership role. He sold life insurance for a living.

In 1952, Lee was tapped at the Republican National Convention to give a seconding speech for the nomination of Robert Taft against Dwight Eisenhower. This marked the first time a Black politician had addressed a national political convention in decades.

Lee died in the late 1960s.

The Police Museum

The Police Museum is a popular attraction on Beale Street.

Keith Richards

Larry Carlton

You never know who will show up at B. B. King's Blues Club.

Photos by Bob Guthridge © 1997

Bernard and Luther Allison

Kenny Wayne Shepard

Photos by Bob Guthridge © 1997

Leo "Tater Red" Allred

Leo "Tater Red" Allred is one of the many Beale Street store owners.

Inside the Rum Boogie Cafe

The fine art of restaurant decoration receives its ultimate challenge in many Beale Street pubs. The Rum Boogie is no exception. The rough-cut lumber siding is graced with record labels, beer advertisements, pieces of guitars and other musical equipment, and a host of other items that have helped make Beale Street an entertainment center.

Acknowledgements

We would like to thank Ernest and Richard at Withers Photography for all their help on this project. Many days were spent researching the photographs that were used in the book and because of all this time we spent together, we came to know both of these gentlemen very well. We are proud to say that both Ernest and Richard are much more than just photographers, they are our friends.

We would also like to thank the folks at Barking Dog Productions and Mid-South Concerts for all their help during the Beale Street International Music Festival.

A very special thanks to the many shop and club owners, managers and employees for all their assistance in helping us obtain some wonderful photographs.

"Big John" and Bob at B.B. King's were instrumental in getting us what we needed, along with Cliff and Lisa at the Hard Rock Cafe and Leo "Tater Red" Allred at Tater Red's.

And finally a special thanks to the citizens of Memphis for their gracious hospitality.